NICKELODEON

降去神通

AVATAR

THE LAST AIRBENDER

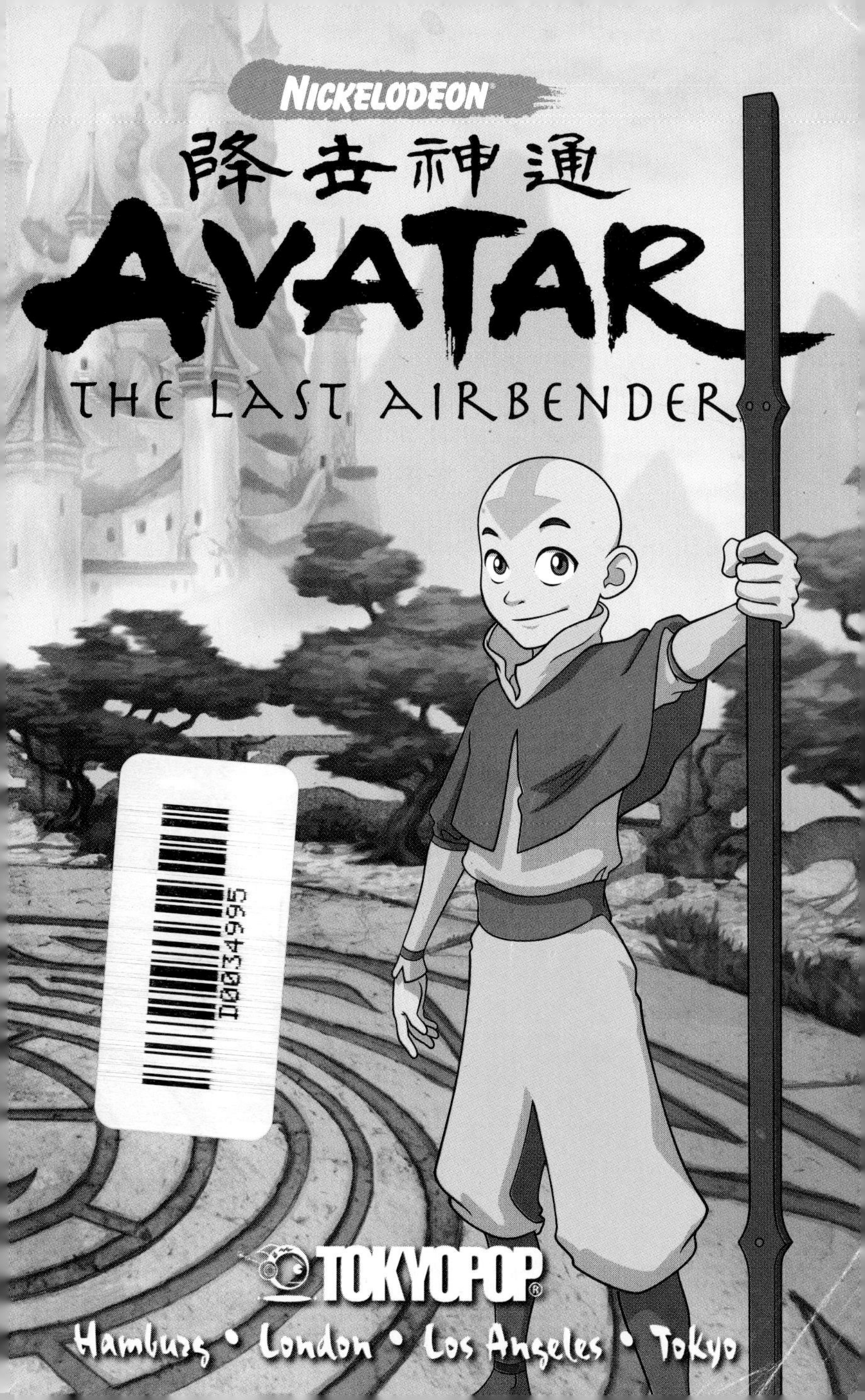

TOKYOPOP

Hamburg • London • Los Angeles • Tokyo

Editor - Zachary Rau
Contributing Editor - Robert Langhorn
Graphic Designer and Letterer - Tomás Montalvo-Lagos
Cover Designer - Jorge Negrete
Graphic Artists - Anna Kernbaum, John Lo, Louis Csontos and Monalisa J. de Asis

Digital Imaging Manager - Chris Buford
Production Managers - Jennifer Miller and Mutsumi Miyazaki
Senior Designer - Anna Kernbaum
Senior Editor - Elizabeth Hurchalla
Managing Editor - Lindsey Johnston
VP of Production - Ron Klamert
Publisher & Editor in Chief - Mike Kiley
President & C.O.O. - John Parker
C.E.O. - Stuart Levy

E-mail: info@TOKYOPOP.com
Come visit us online at www.TOKYOPOP.com

A ⊙**TOKYOPOP** Cine-Manga® Book
TOKYOPOP Inc.
5900 Wilshire Blvd., Suite 2000
Los Angeles, CA 90036

Avatar: The Last Airbender Volume 1

© 2006 Viacom International Inc. All Rights Reserved.
Nickelodeon, Avatar and all related titles, logos and characters are trademarks
of Viacom International Inc.

All rights reserved. No portion of this book may be reproduced or
transmitted in any form or by any means without written permission
from the copyright holders. This Cine-Manga book is a work of fiction.
Any resemblance to actual events or locales or persons,
living or dead, is entirely coincidental.

ISBN: 1-59532-891-2

First TOKYOPOP® printing: February 2006

10 9 8 7 6 5 4 3 2 1

Printed in Canada

NICKELODEON

降去神通

AVATAR

THE LAST AIRBENDER™

CREATED BY
MICHAEL DANTE DIMARTINO &
BRYAN KONIETZKO

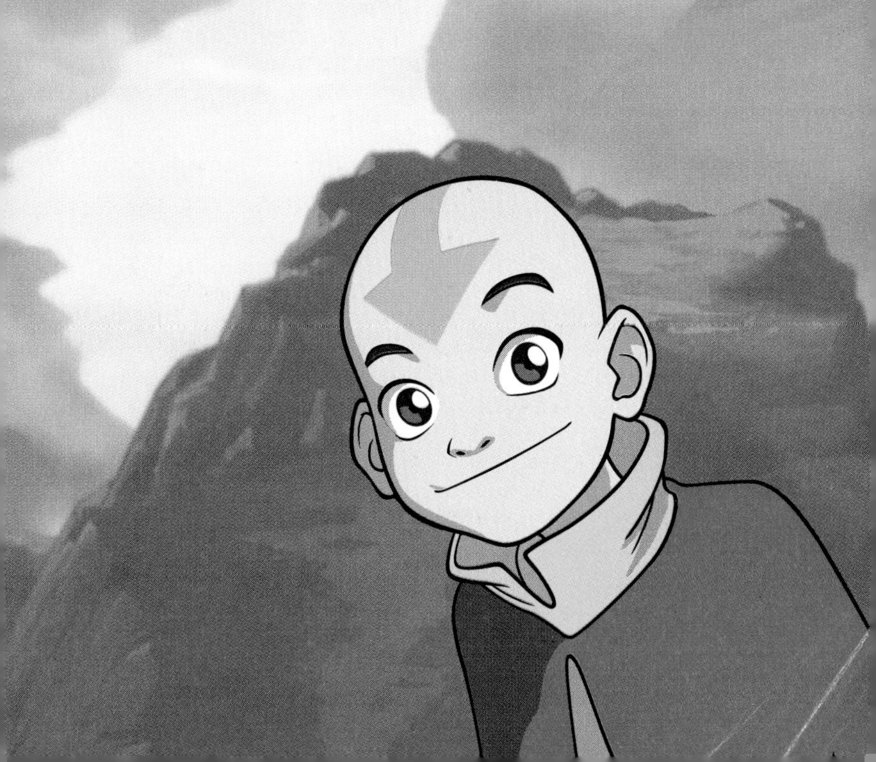

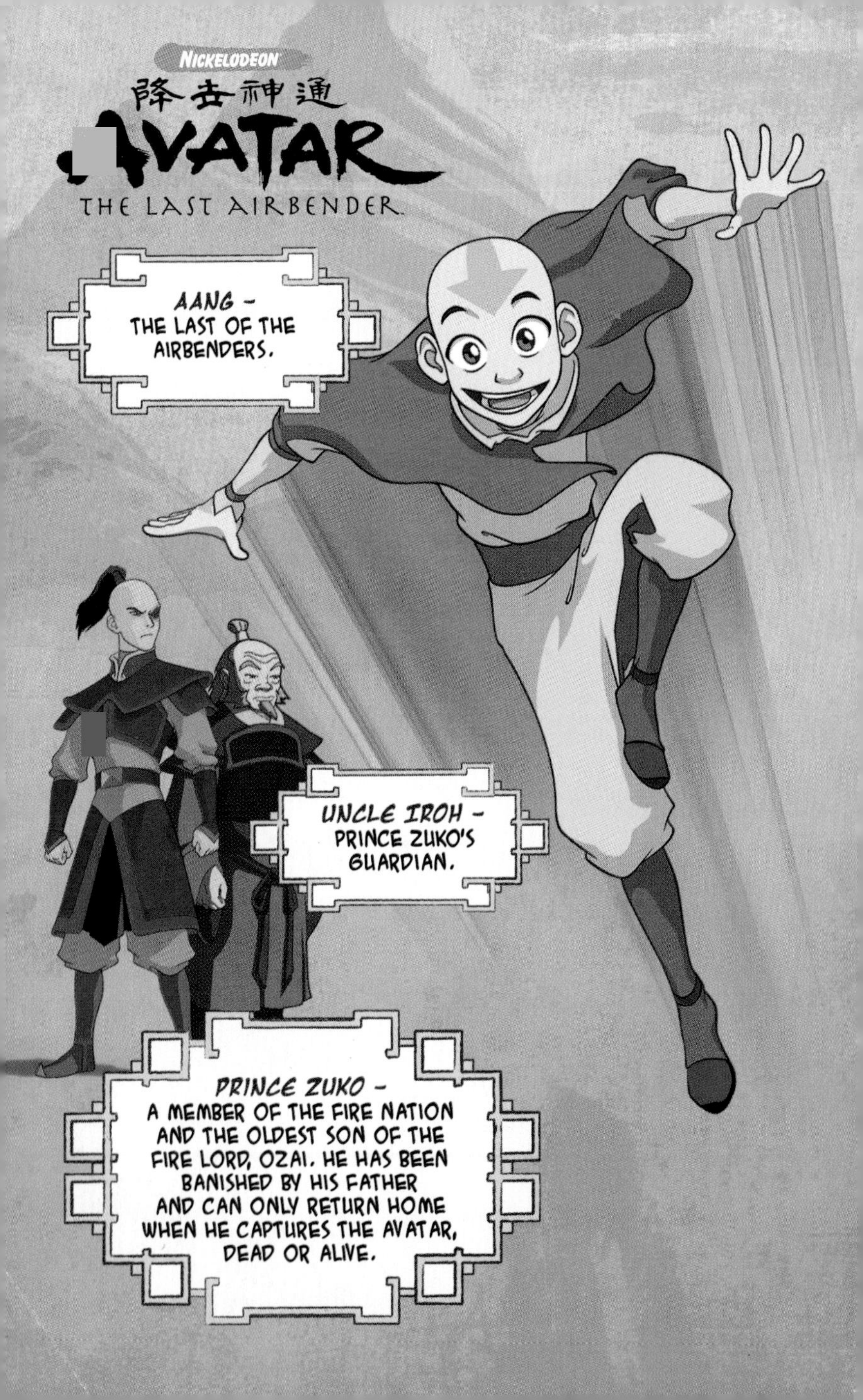
NICKELODEON
降世神通
AVATAR
THE LAST AIRBENDER
AANG – THE LAST OF THE AIRBENDERS.
UNCLE IROH – PRINCE ZUKO'S GUARDIAN.
PRINCE ZUKO – A MEMBER OF THE FIRE NATION AND THE OLDEST SON OF THE FIRE LORD, OZAI. HE HAS BEEN BANISHED BY HIS FATHER AND CAN ONLY RETURN HOME WHEN HE CAPTURES THE AVATAR, DEAD OR ALIVE.

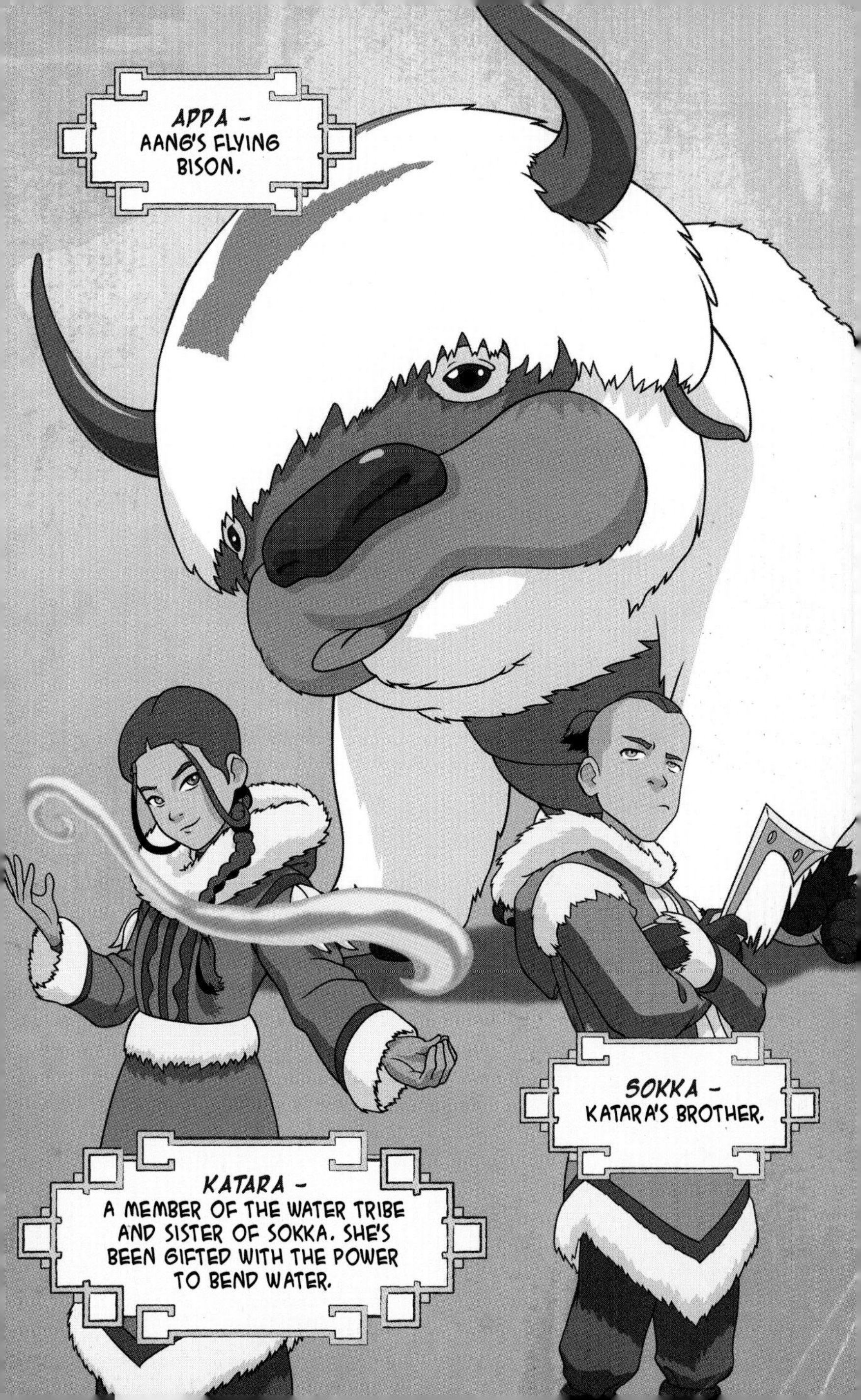
APPA - AANG'S FLYING BISON.
SOKKA - KATARA'S BROTHER.
KATARA - A MEMBER OF THE WATER TRIBE AND SISTER OF SOKKA. SHE'S BEEN GIFTED WITH THE POWER TO BEND WATER.

NICKELODEON

降击神通

AVATAR

THE LAST AIRBENDER.

VOL.1 CONTENTS

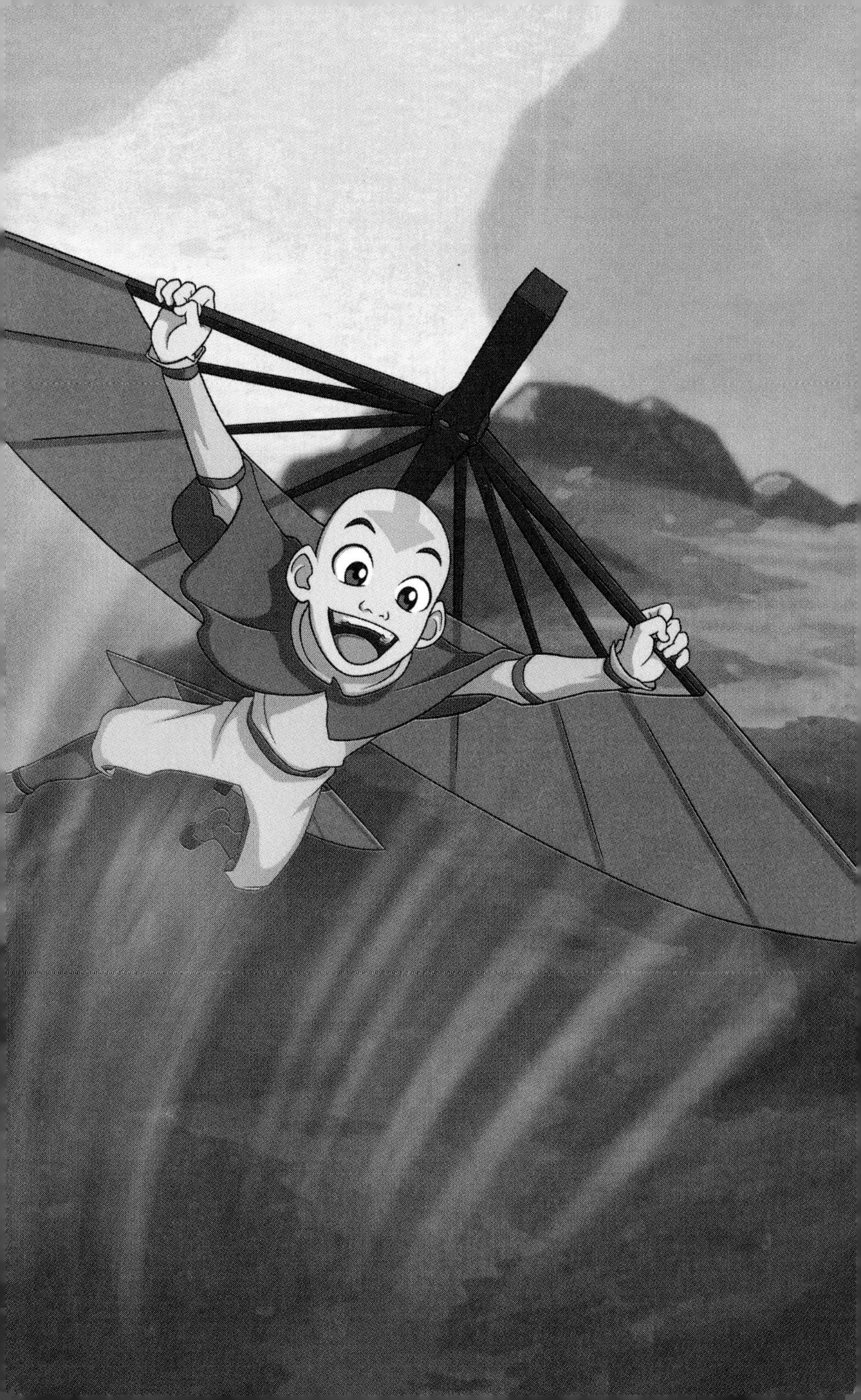

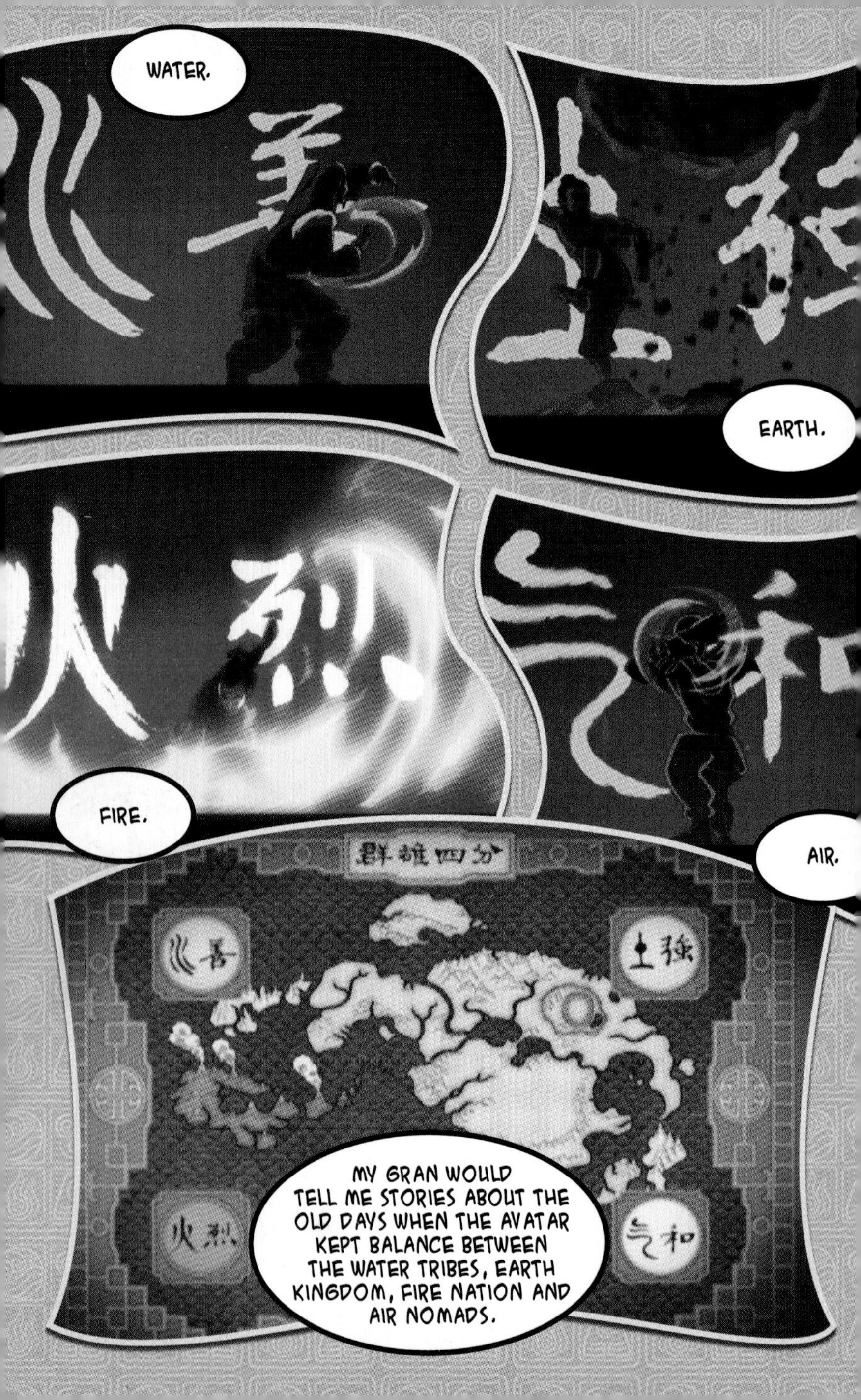

WATER.
EARTH.
FIRE.
AIR.
MY GRAN WOULD TELL ME STORIES ABOUT THE OLD DAYS WHEN THE AVATAR KEPT BALANCE BETWEEN THE WATER TRIBES, EARTH KINGDOM, FIRE NATION AND AIR NOMADS.

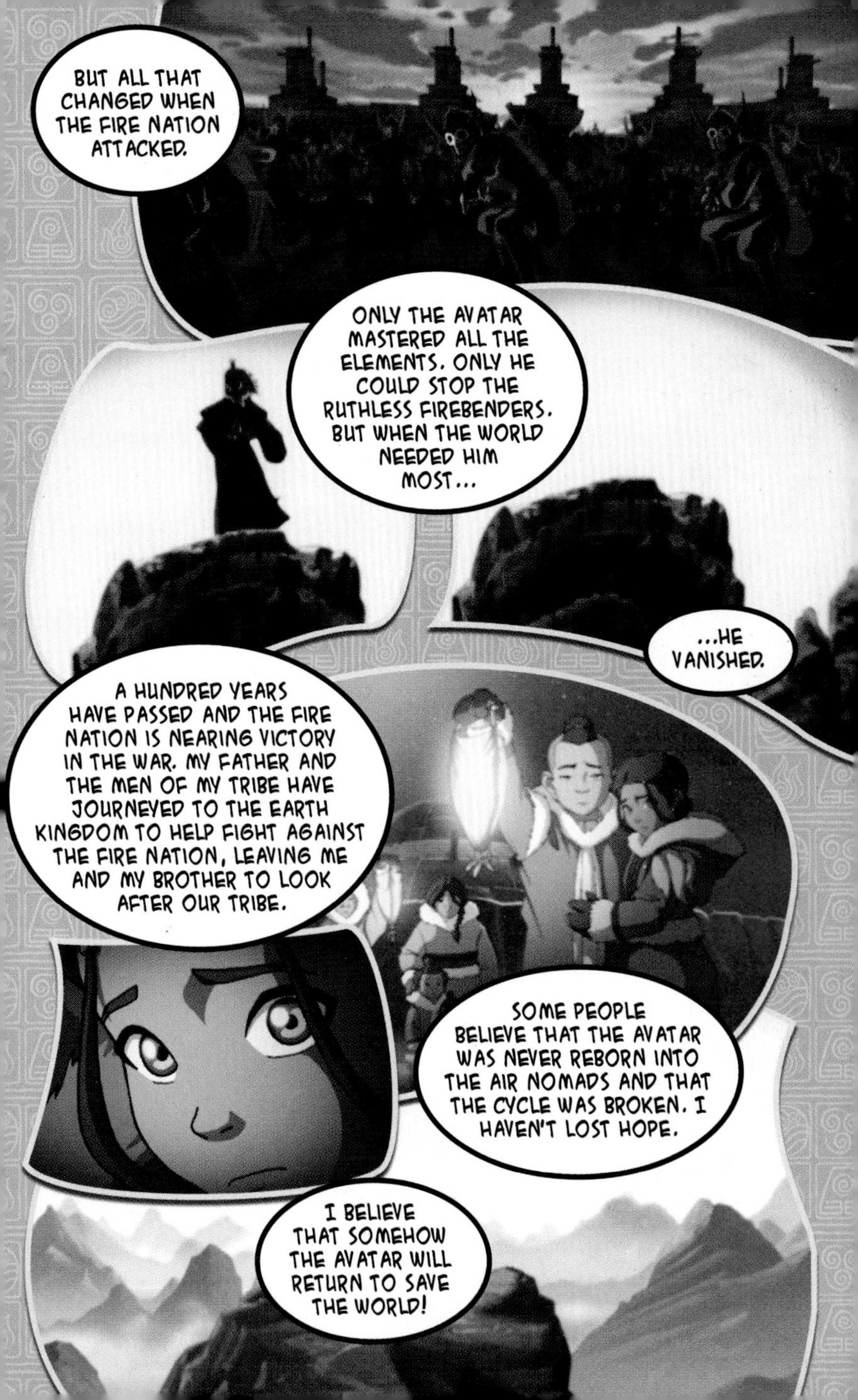
BUT ALL THAT CHANGED WHEN THE FIRE NATION ATTACKED.
ONLY THE AVATAR MASTERED ALL THE ELEMENTS. ONLY HE COULD STOP THE RUTHLESS FIREBENDERS. BUT WHEN THE WORLD NEEDED HIM MOST...
...HE VANISHED.
A HUNDRED YEARS HAVE PASSED AND THE FIRE NATION IS NEARING VICTORY IN THE WAR. MY FATHER AND THE MEN OF MY TRIBE HAVE JOURNEYED TO THE EARTH KINGDOM TO HELP FIGHT AGAINST THE FIRE NATION, LEAVING ME AND MY BROTHER TO LOOK AFTER OUR TRIBE.
SOME PEOPLE BELIEVE THAT THE AVATAR WAS NEVER REBORN INTO THE AIR NOMADS AND THAT THE CYCLE WAS BROKEN. I HAVEN'T LOST HOPE.
I BELIEVE THAT SOMEHOW THE AVATAR WILL RETURN TO SAVE THE WORLD!

BOOK ONE: WATER

THE BOY IN THE ICEBERG

WRITTEN BY
MICHAEL DANTE DIMARTINO
& BRYAN KONIETZKO

ADDITIONAL WRITING BY
AARON EHASZ, PETER GOLDFINGER
AND JOSH STOLBERG

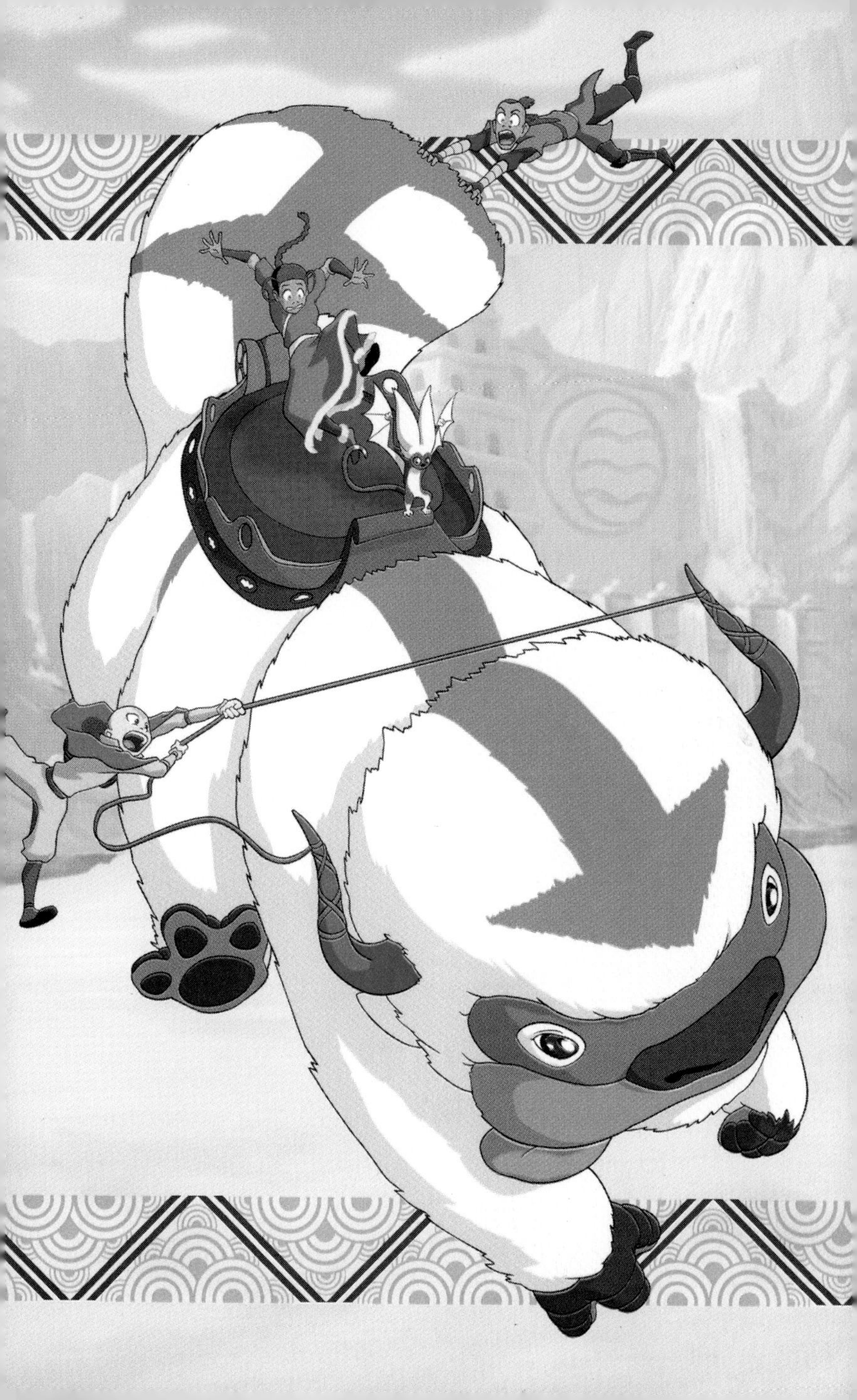

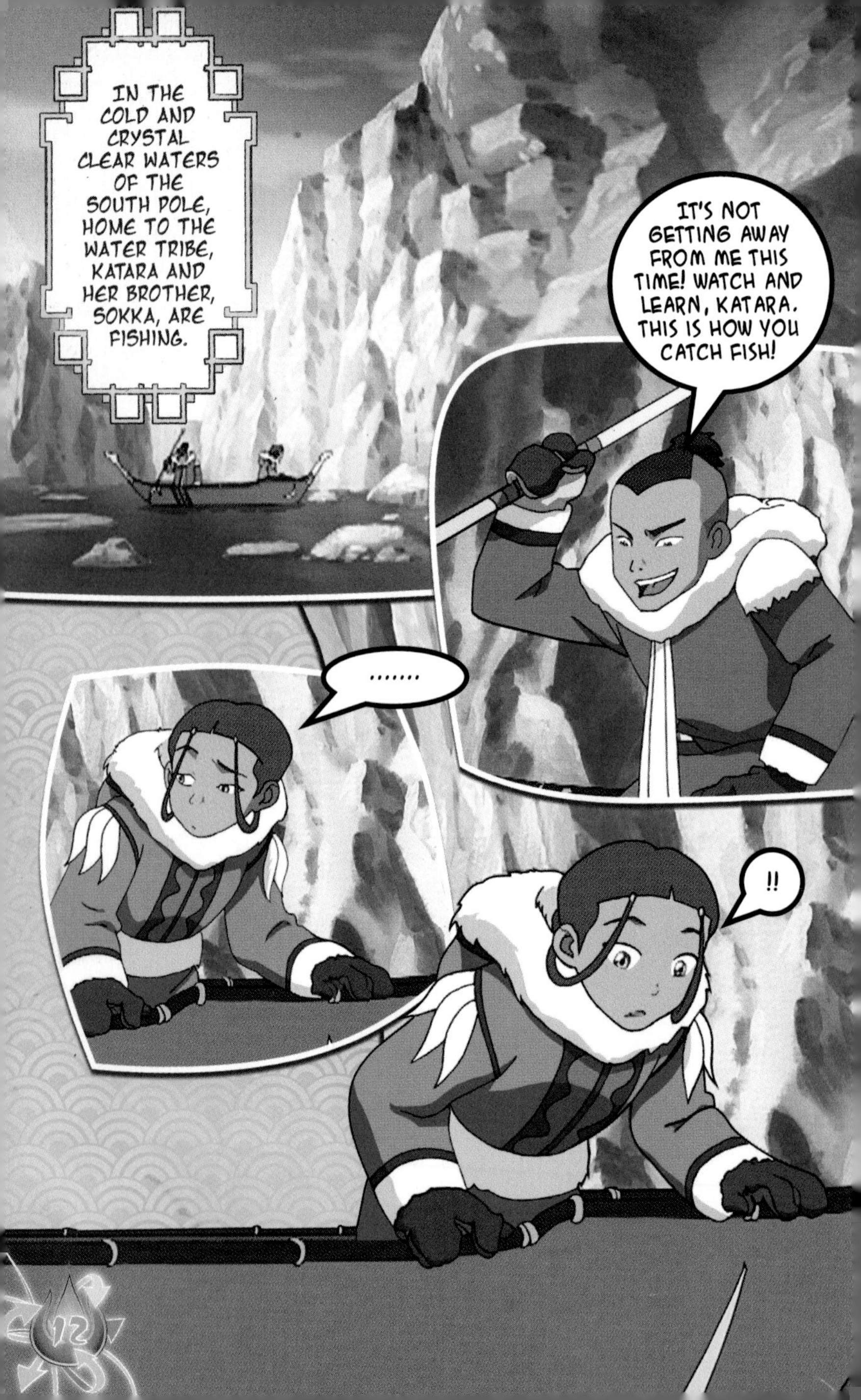

IN THE COLD AND CRYSTAL CLEAR WATERS OF THE SOUTH POLE, HOME TO THE WATER TRIBE, KATARA AND HER BROTHER, SOKKA, ARE FISHING.
IT'S NOT GETTING AWAY FROM ME THIS TIME! WATCH AND LEARN, KATARA. THIS IS HOW YOU CATCH FISH!
....
!!

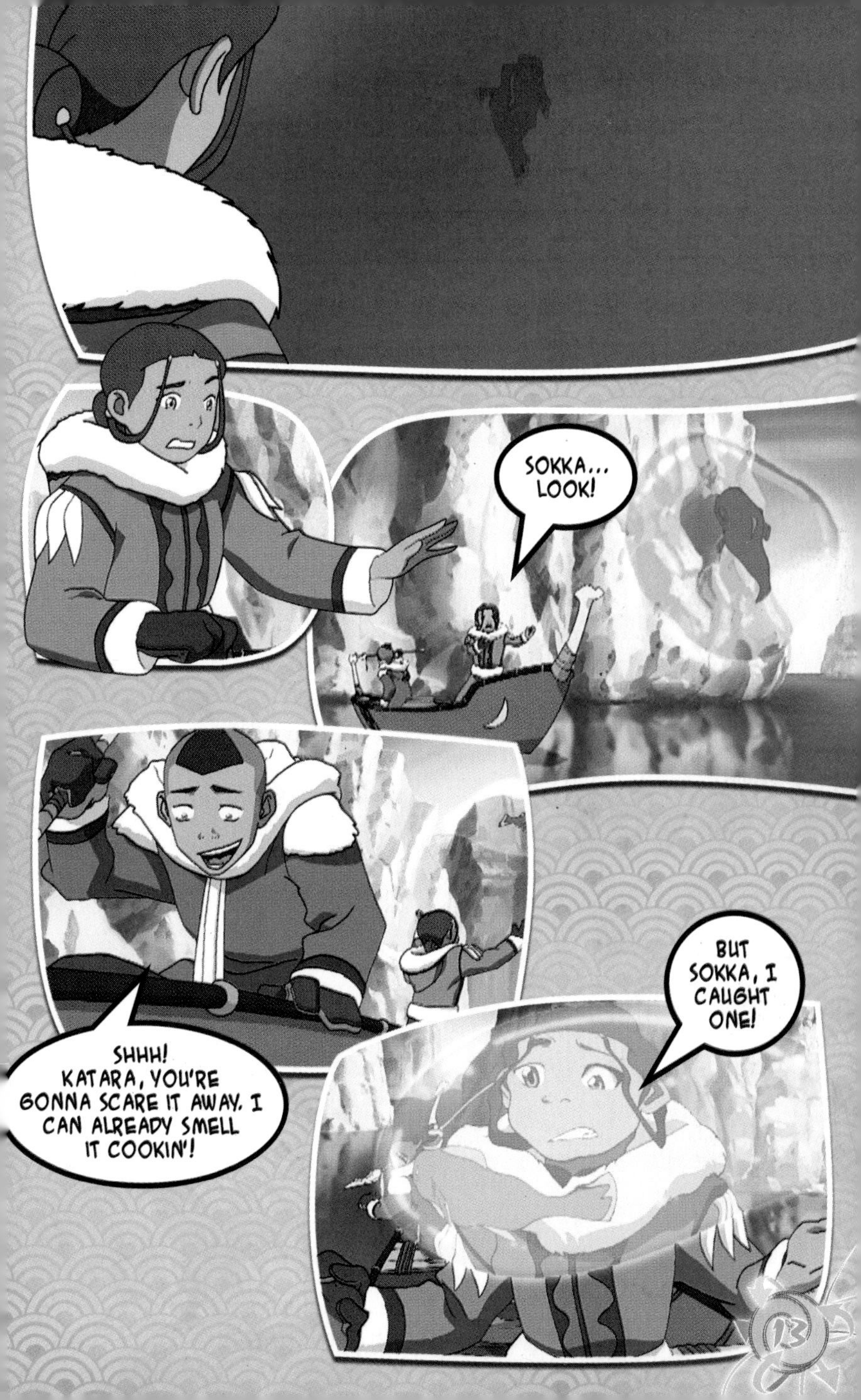
SOKKA... LOOK!
SHHH! KATARA, YOU'RE GONNA SCARE IT AWAY. I CAN ALREADY SMELL IT COOKIN'!
BUT SOKKA, I CAUGHT ONE!
13

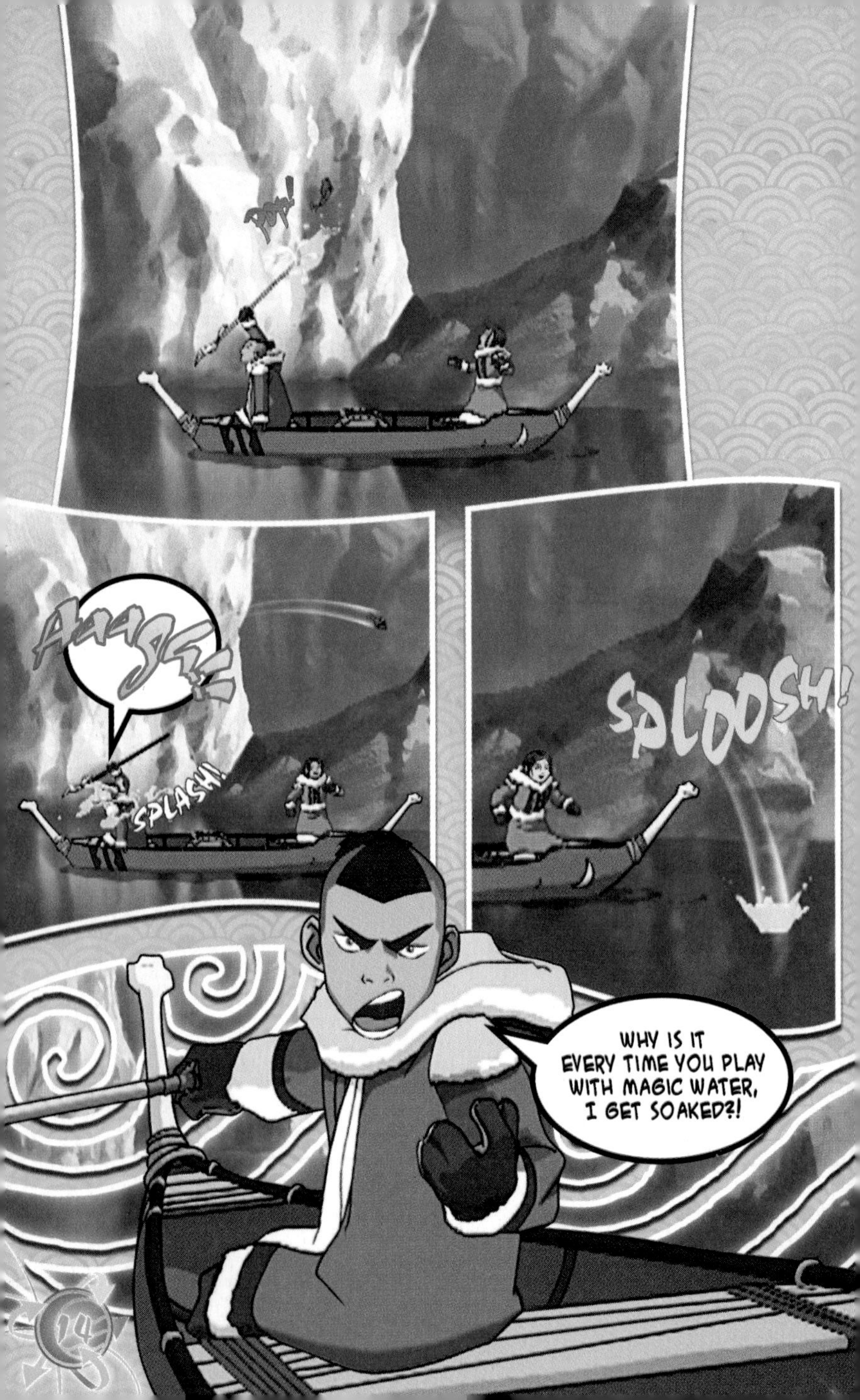
AAAGH!!
SPLASH!
SPLOOSH!
WHY IS IT
EVERY TIME YOU PLAY
WITH MAGIC WATER,
I GET SOAKED?!

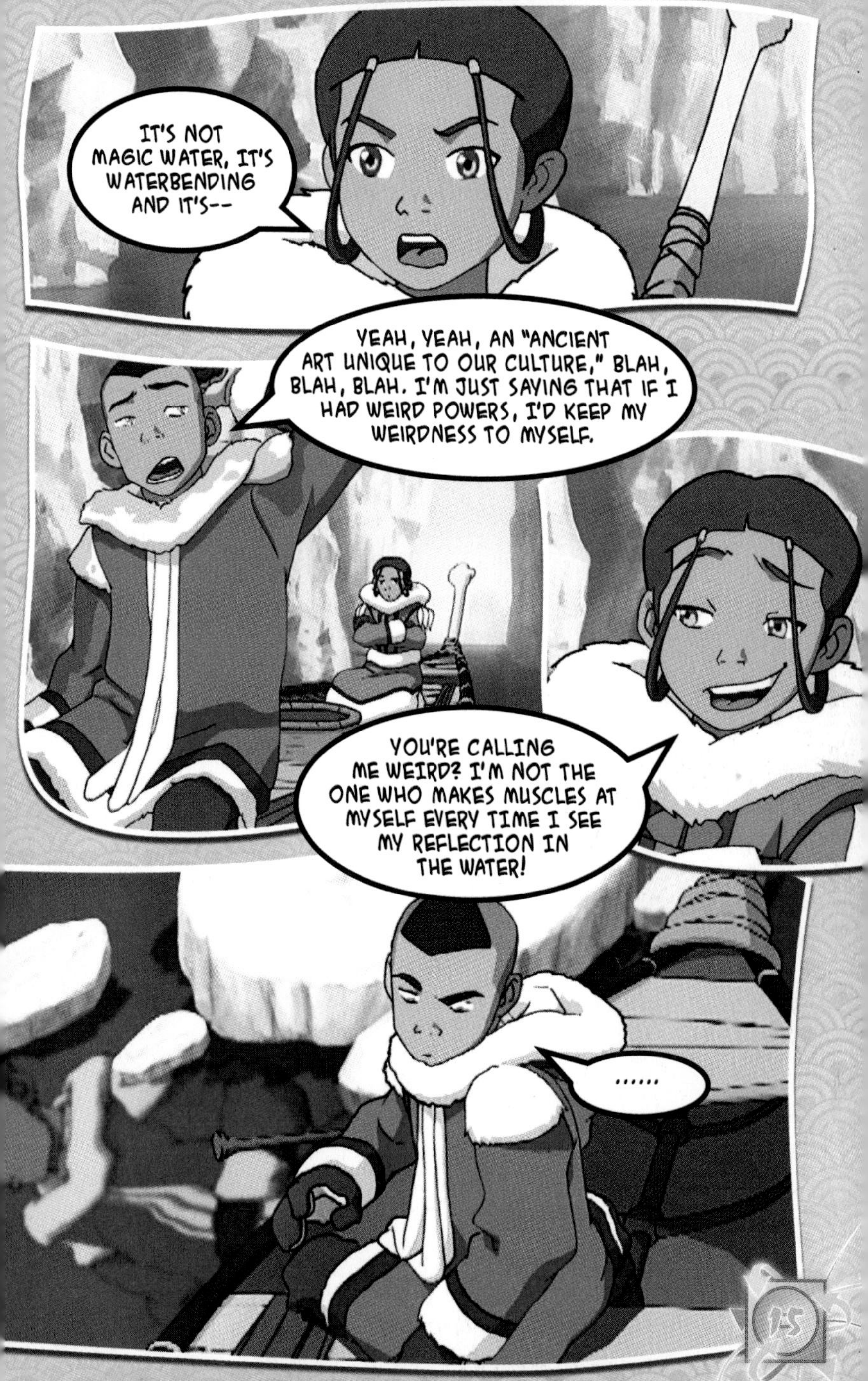
IT'S NOT MAGIC WATER, IT'S WATERBENDING AND IT'S--
YEAH, YEAH, AN "ANCIENT ART UNIQUE TO OUR CULTURE," BLAH, BLAH, BLAH. I'M JUST SAYING THAT IF I HAD WEIRD POWERS, I'D KEEP MY WEIRDNESS TO MYSELF.
YOU'RE CALLING ME WEIRD? I'M NOT THE ONE WHO MAKES MUSCLES AT MYSELF EVERY TIME I SEE MY REFLECTION IN THE WATER!
......

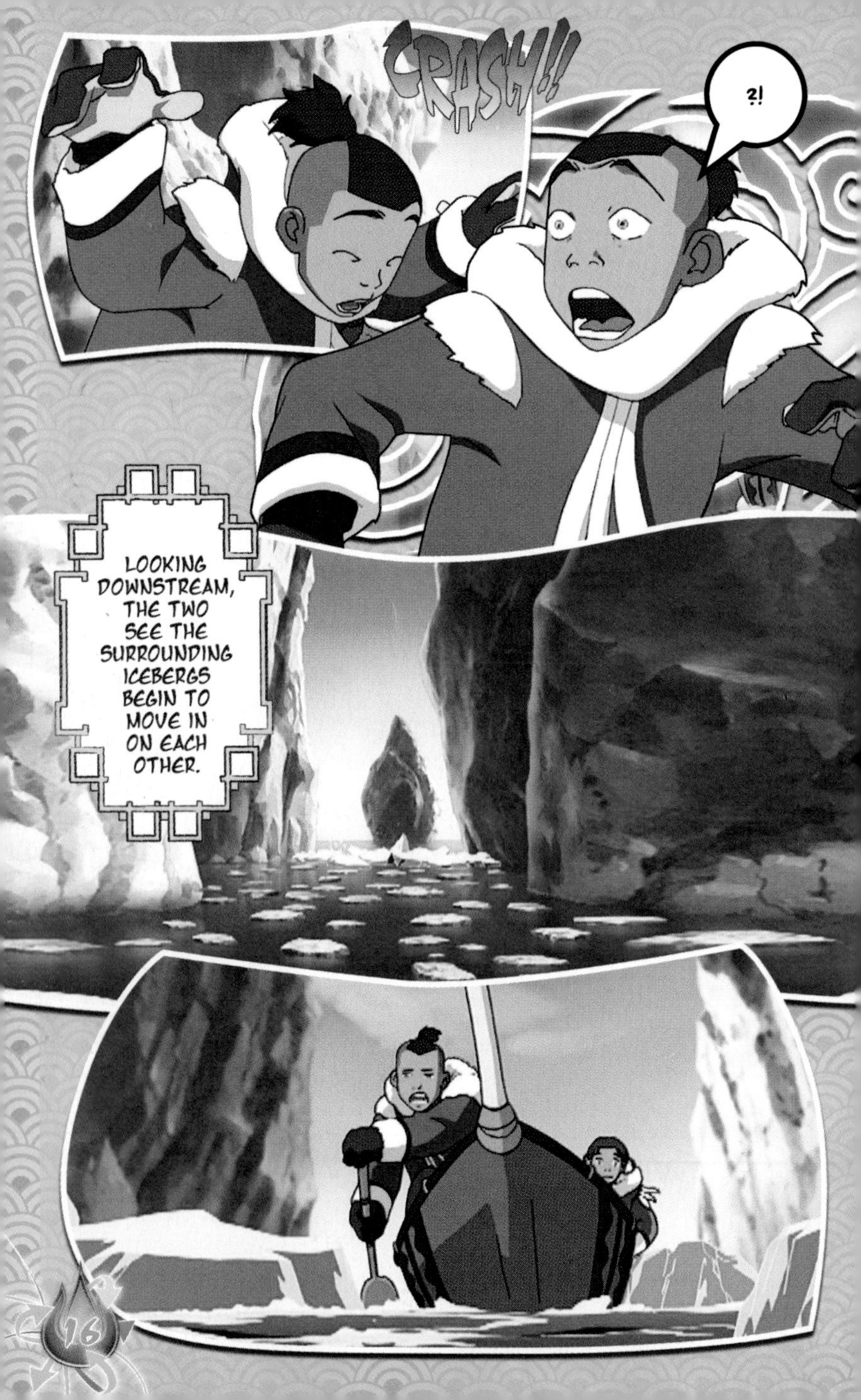
CRASH!!
?!
LOOKING DOWNSTREAM, THE TWO SEE THE SURROUNDING ICEBERGS BEGIN TO MOVE IN ON EACH OTHER.

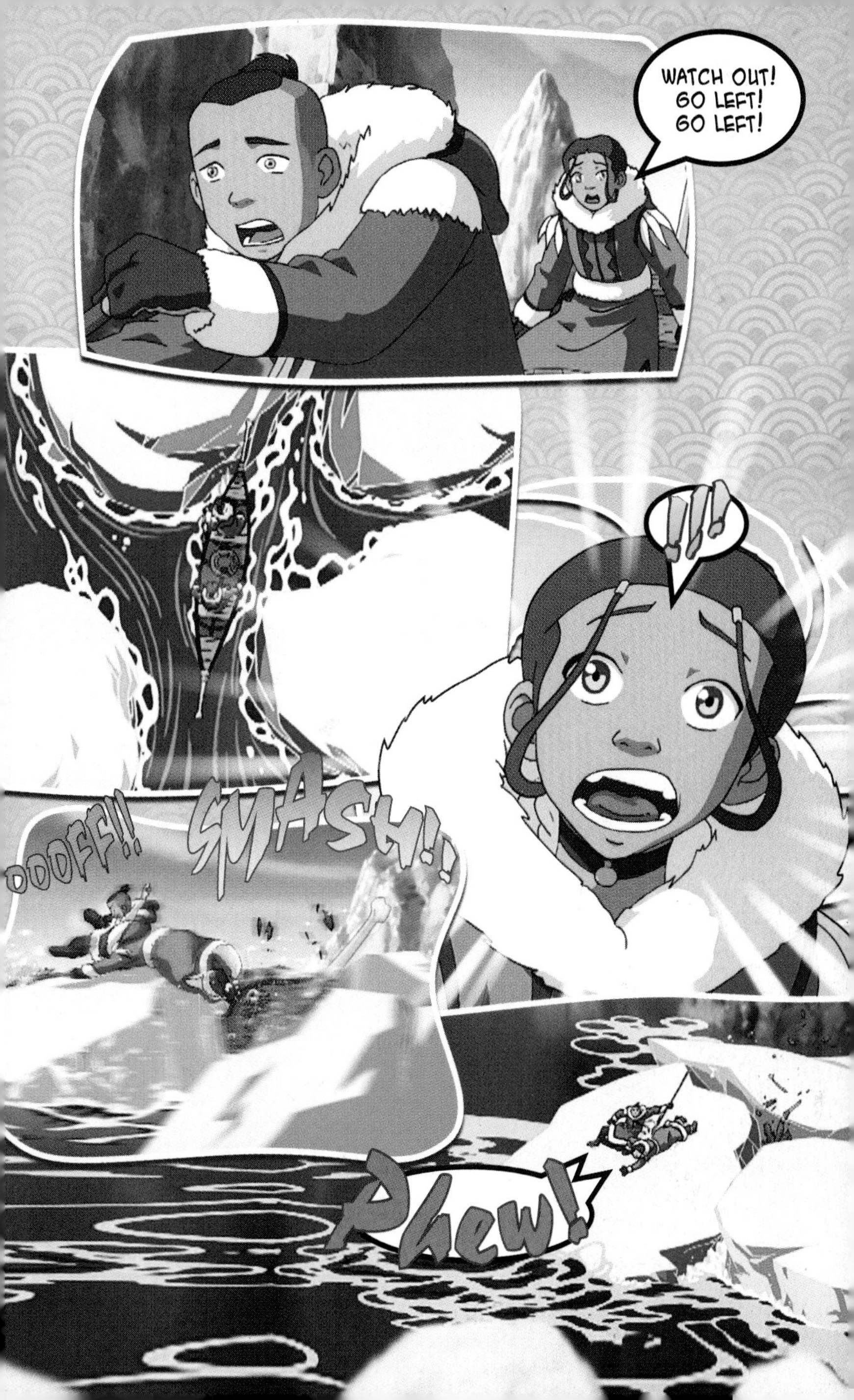
WATCH OUT! GO LEFT! GO LEFT!
!!
OOOFF!!
SMASH!!
Phew!

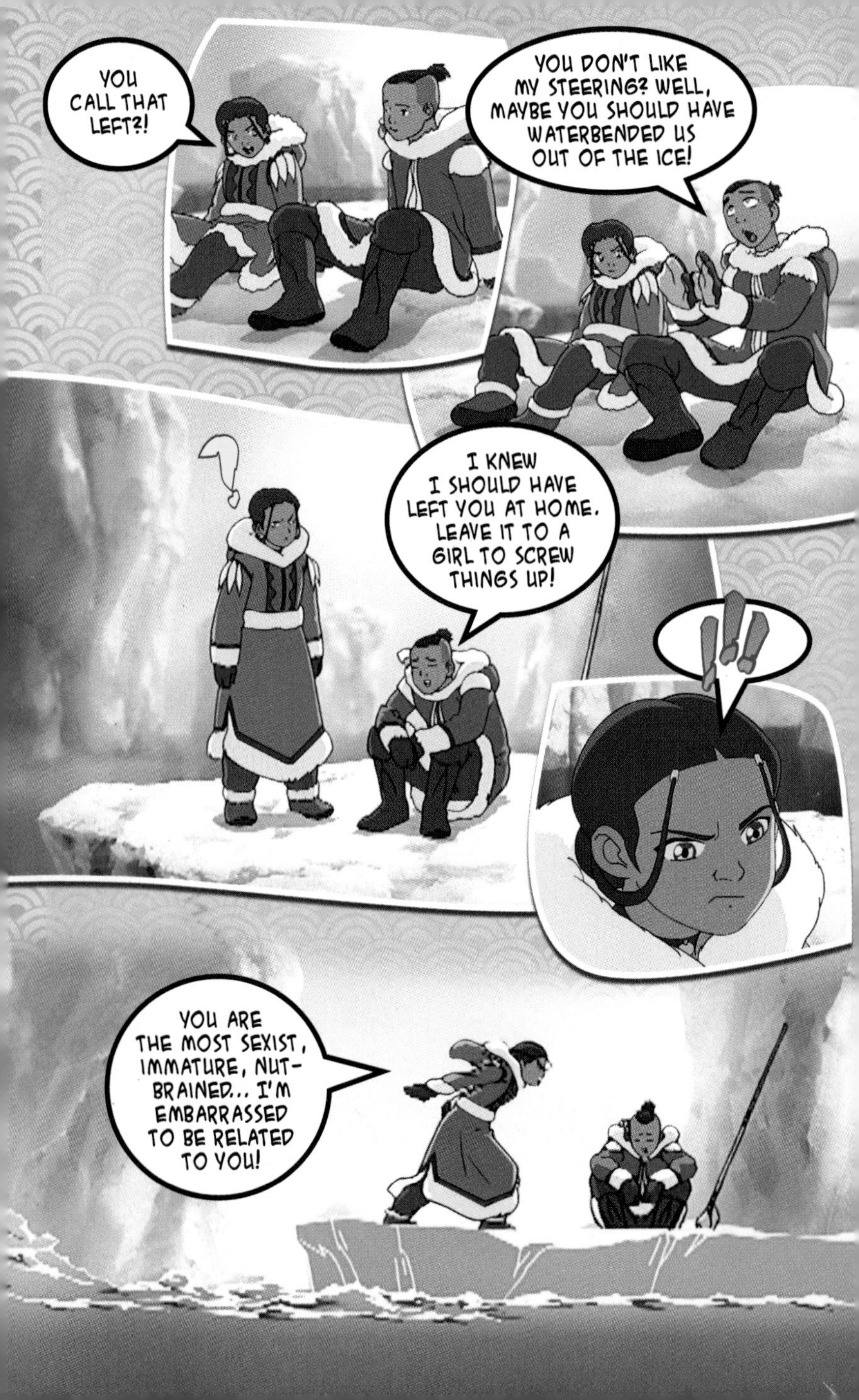
YOU CALL THAT LEFT?!
YOU DON'T LIKE MY STEERING? WELL, MAYBE YOU SHOULD HAVE WATERBENDED US OUT OF THE ICE!
I KNEW I SHOULD HAVE LEFT YOU AT HOME. LEAVE IT TO A GIRL TO SCREW THINGS UP!
YOU ARE THE MOST SEXIST, IMMATURE, NUT-BRAINED... I'M EMBARRASSED TO BE RELATED TO YOU!

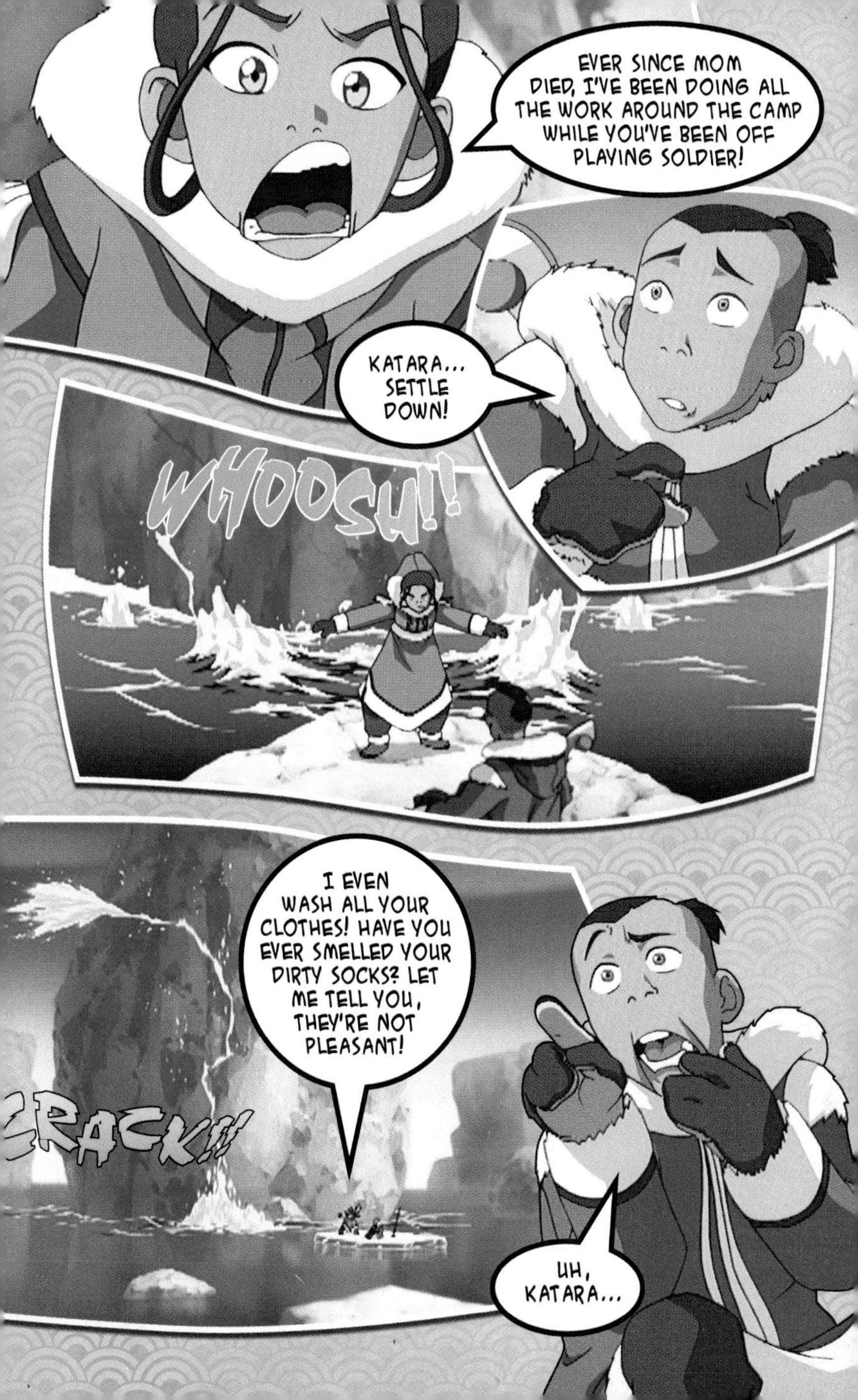
EVER SINCE MOM DIED, I'VE BEEN DOING ALL THE WORK AROUND THE CAMP WHILE YOU'VE BEEN OFF PLAYING SOLDIER!
KATARA... SETTLE DOWN!
WHOOSH!!
CRACK!!
I EVEN WASH ALL YOUR CLOTHES! HAVE YOU EVER SMELLED YOUR DIRTY SOCKS? LET ME TELL YOU, THEY'RE NOT PLEASANT!
UH, KATARA...

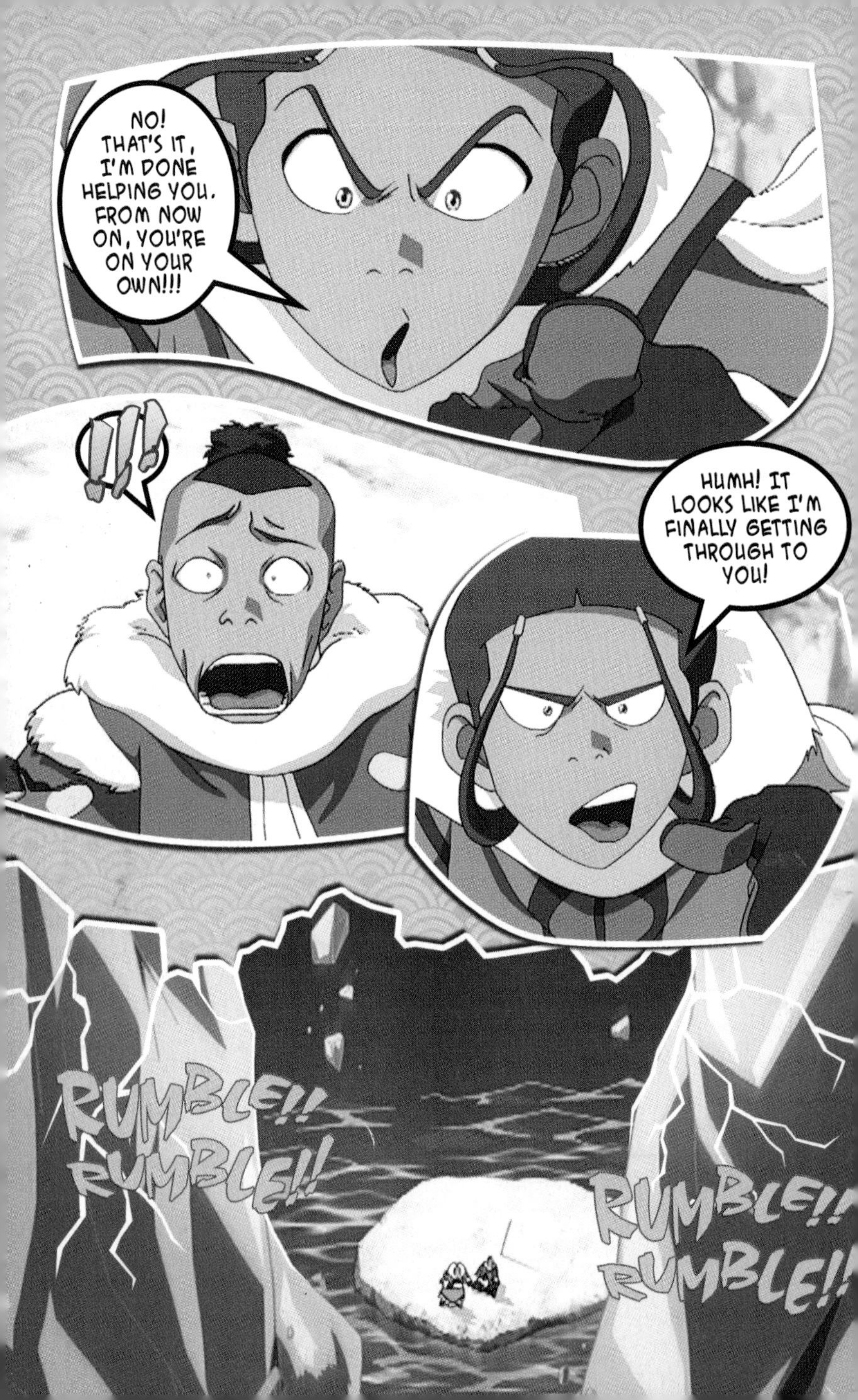
NO! THAT'S IT, I'M DONE HELPING YOU. FROM NOW ON, YOU'RE ON YOUR OWN!!!
!!!
HUMH! IT LOOKS LIKE I'M FINALLY GETTING THROUGH TO YOU!
RUMBLE!! RUMBLE!!
RUMBLE!! RUMBLE!!

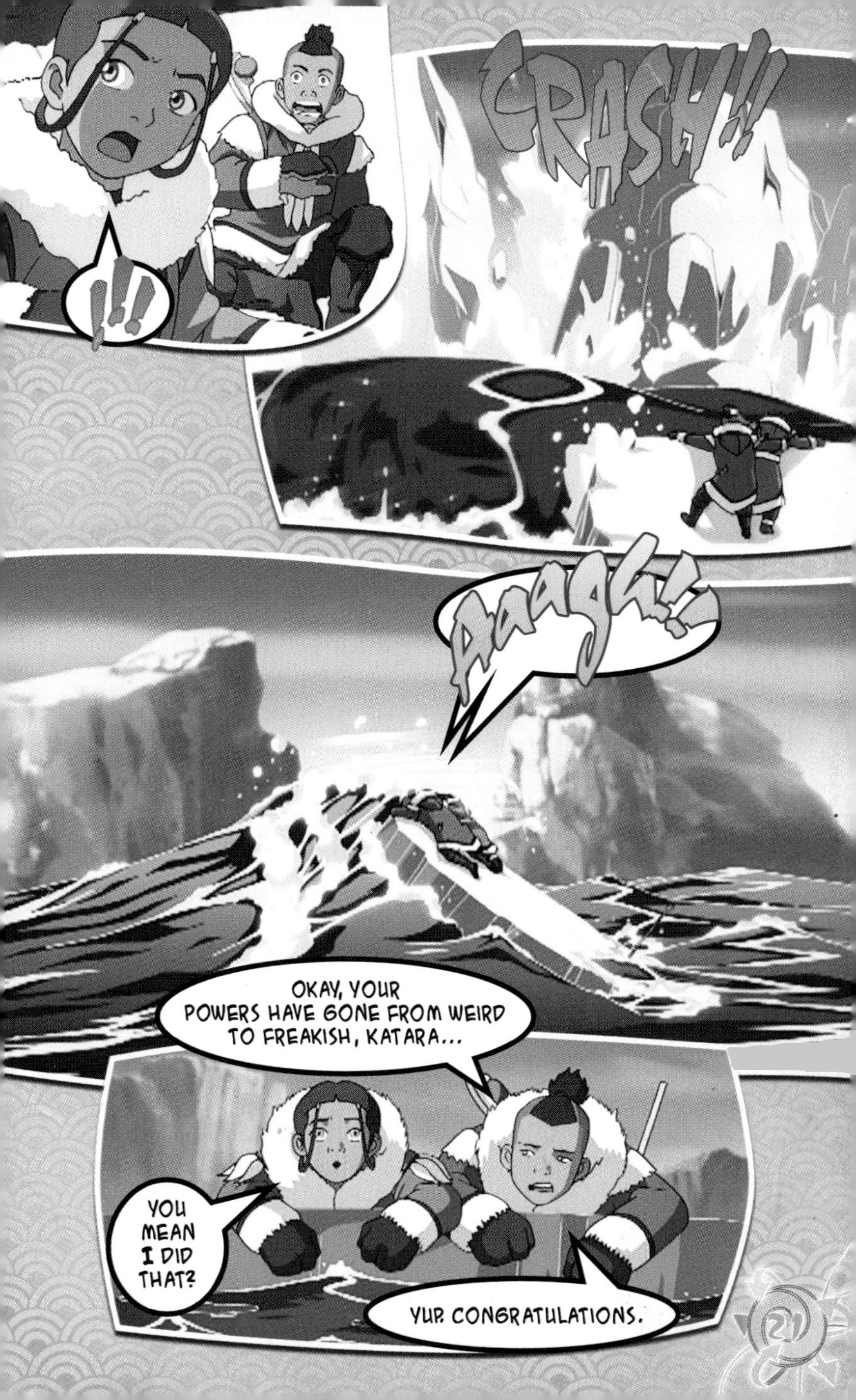
!!
CRASH!!
Aaagh!!
OKAY, YOUR POWERS HAVE GONE FROM WEIRD TO FREAKISH, KATARA...
YOU MEAN I DID THAT?
YUP. CONGRATULATIONS.

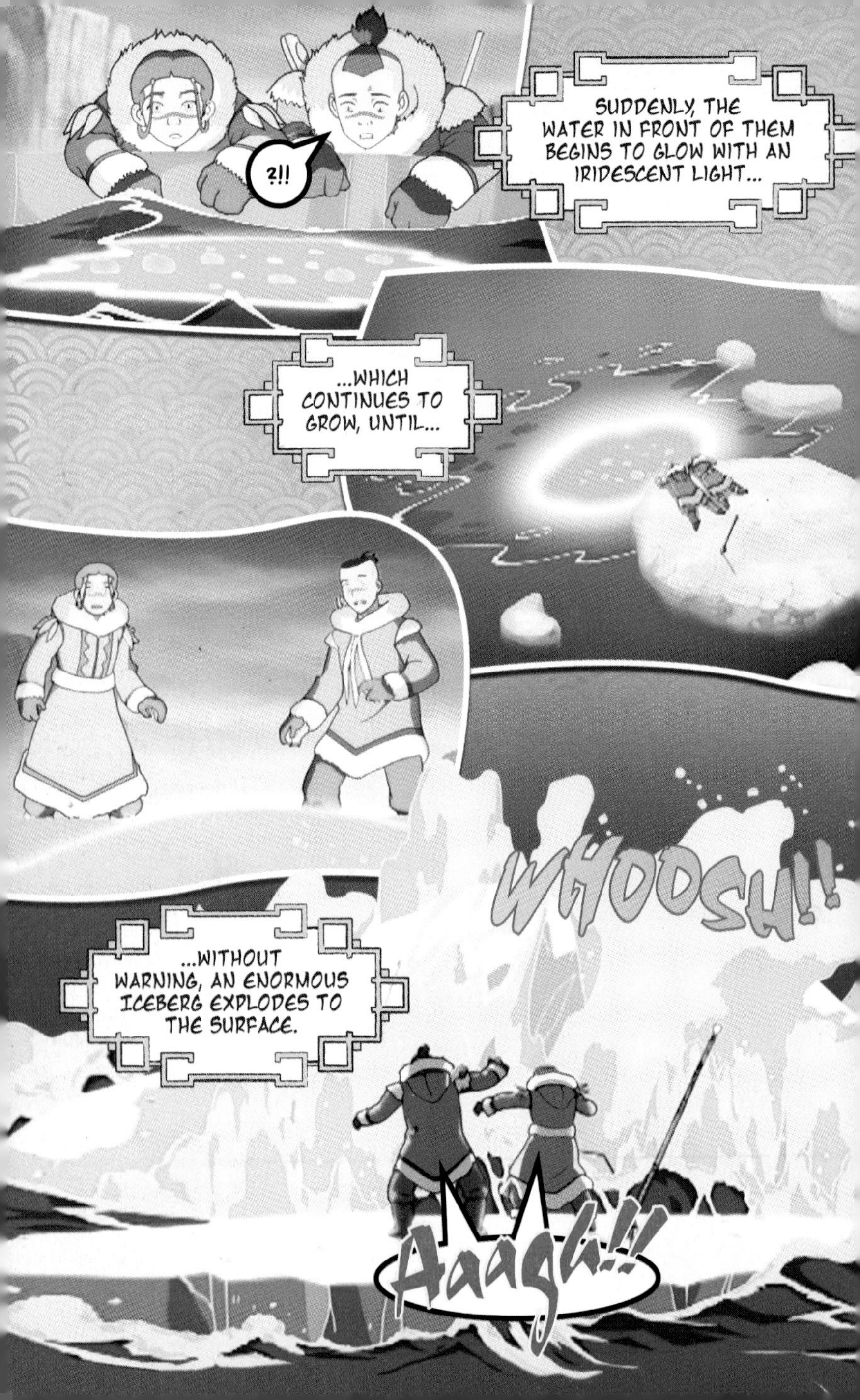
?!!
SUDDENLY, THE WATER IN FRONT OF THEM BEGINS TO GLOW WITH AN IRIDESCENT LIGHT...
...WHICH CONTINUES TO GROW, UNTIL...
WHOOSH!!
...WITHOUT WARNING, AN ENORMOUS ICEBERG EXPLODES TO THE SURFACE.
Aaagh!!

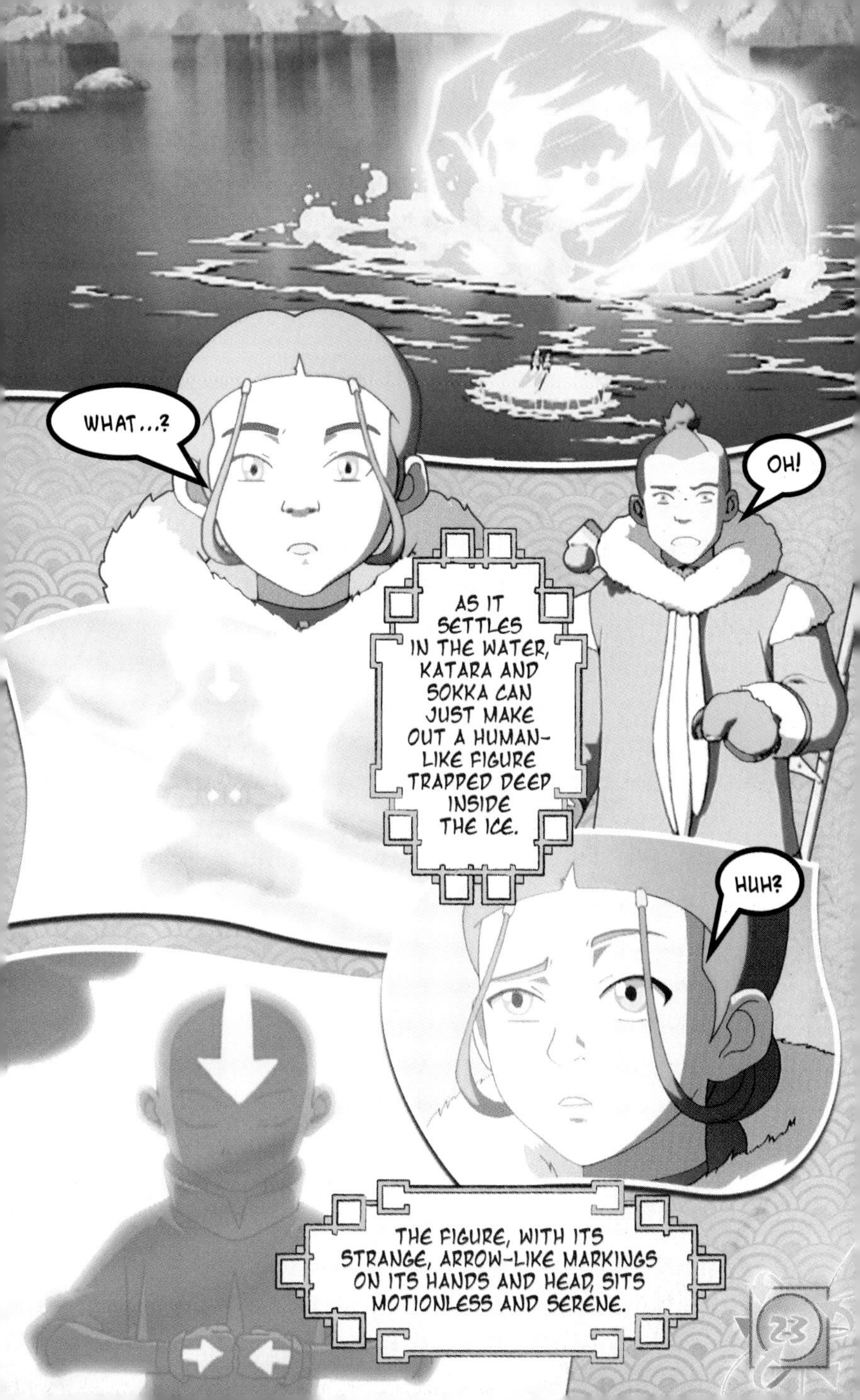
WHAT...?
OH!
AS IT SETTLES IN THE WATER, KATARA AND SOKKA CAN JUST MAKE OUT A HUMAN-LIKE FIGURE TRAPPED DEEP INSIDE THE ICE.
HUH?
THE FIGURE, WITH ITS STRANGE, ARROW-LIKE MARKINGS ON ITS HANDS AND HEAD, SITS MOTIONLESS AND SERENE.

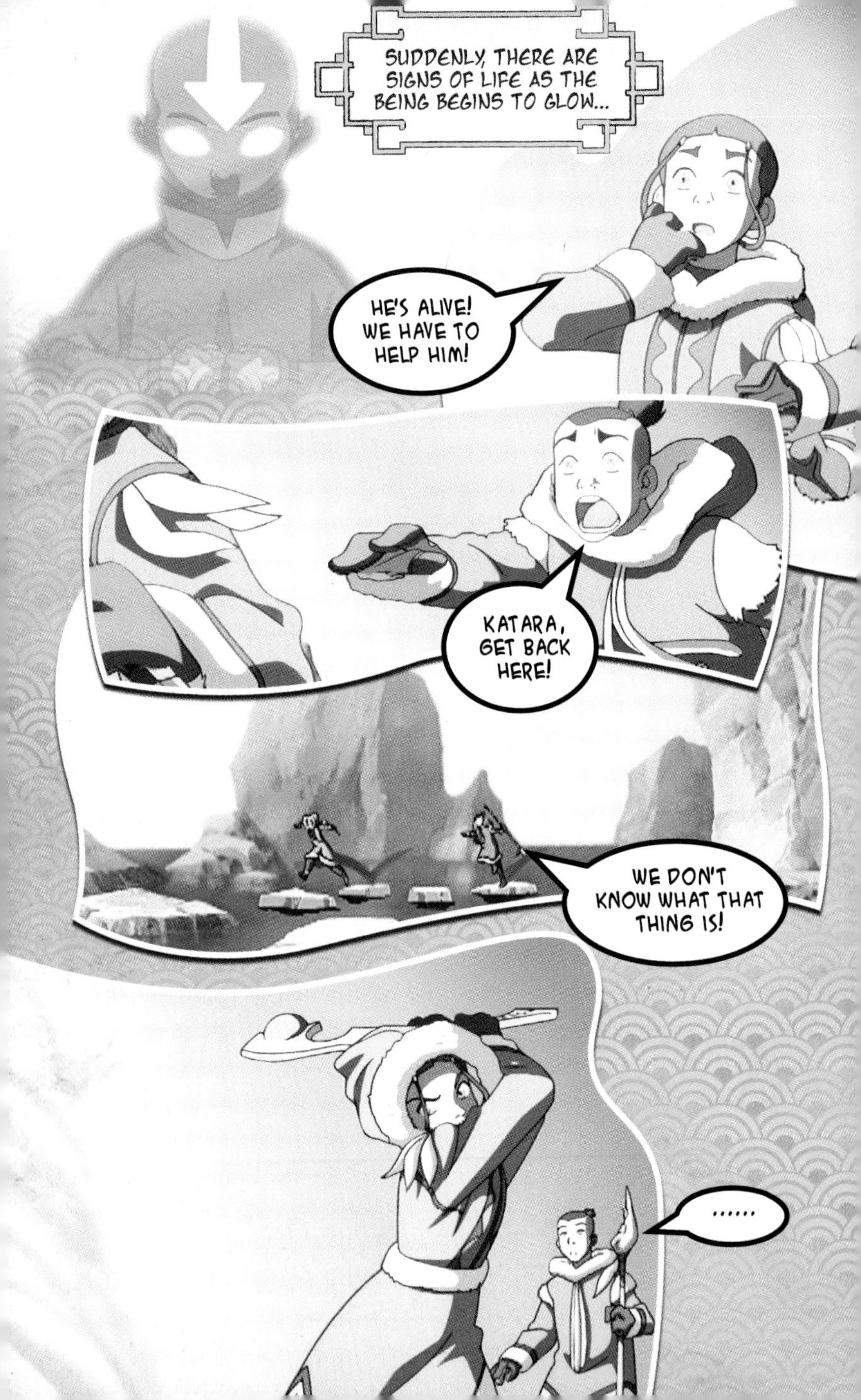
SUDDENLY, THERE ARE SIGNS OF LIFE AS THE BEING BEGINS TO GLOW...
HE'S ALIVE! WE HAVE TO HELP HIM!
KATARA, GET BACK HERE!
WE DON'T KNOW WHAT THAT THING IS!
......

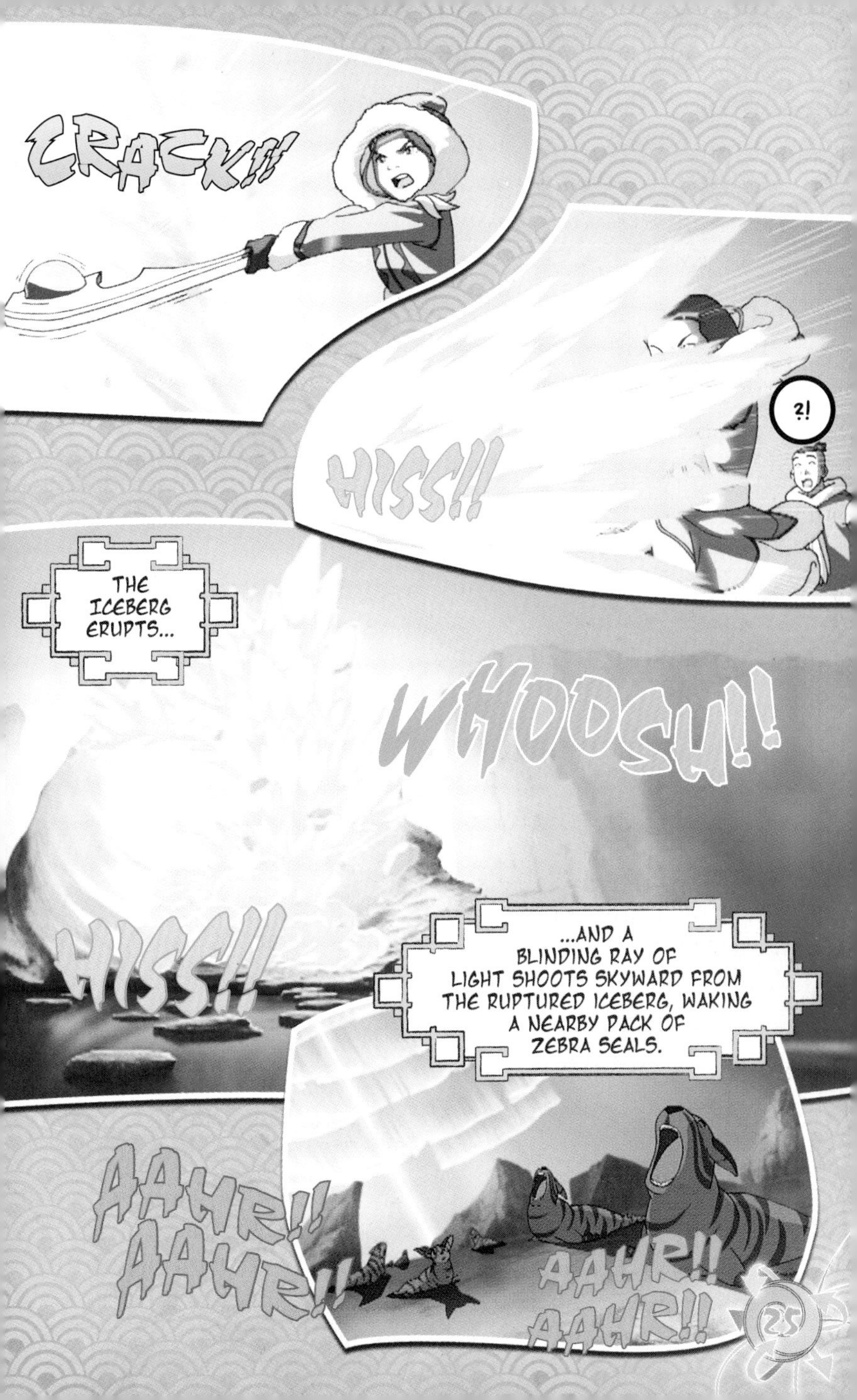
CRACK!!
HISS!!
?!
THE ICEBERG ERUPTS...
WHOOSH!!
HISS!!
...AND A BLINDING RAY OF LIGHT SHOOTS SKYWARD FROM THE RUPTURED ICEBERG, WAKING A NEARBY PACK OF ZEBRA SEALS.
AAHR!! AAHR!!
AAHR!! AAHR!!
25

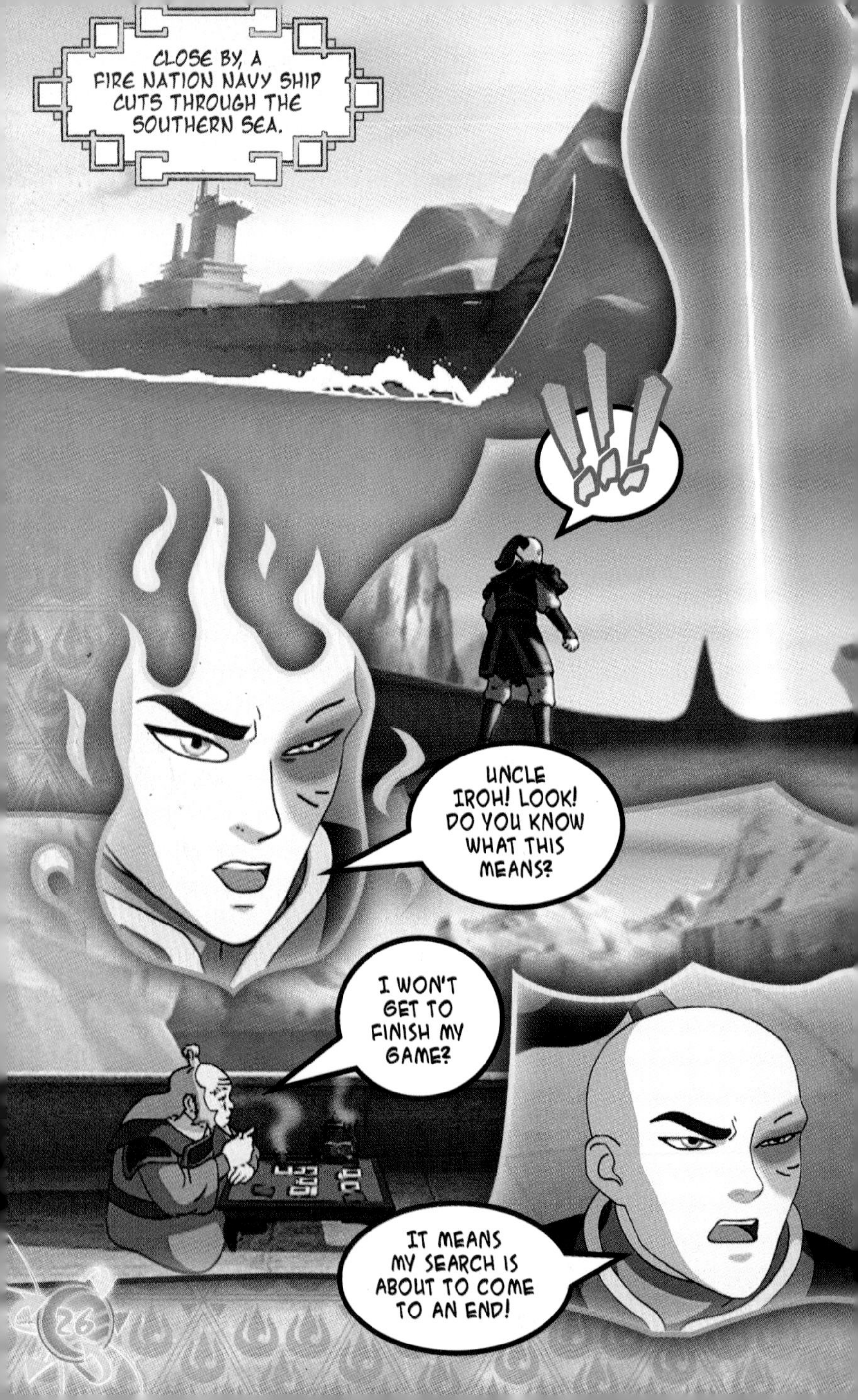

CLOSE BY, A FIRE NATION NAVY SHIP CUTS THROUGH THE SOUTHERN SEA.
!!!
UNCLE IROH! LOOK! DO YOU KNOW WHAT THIS MEANS?
I WON'T GET TO FINISH MY GAME?
IT MEANS MY SEARCH IS ABOUT TO COME TO AN END!

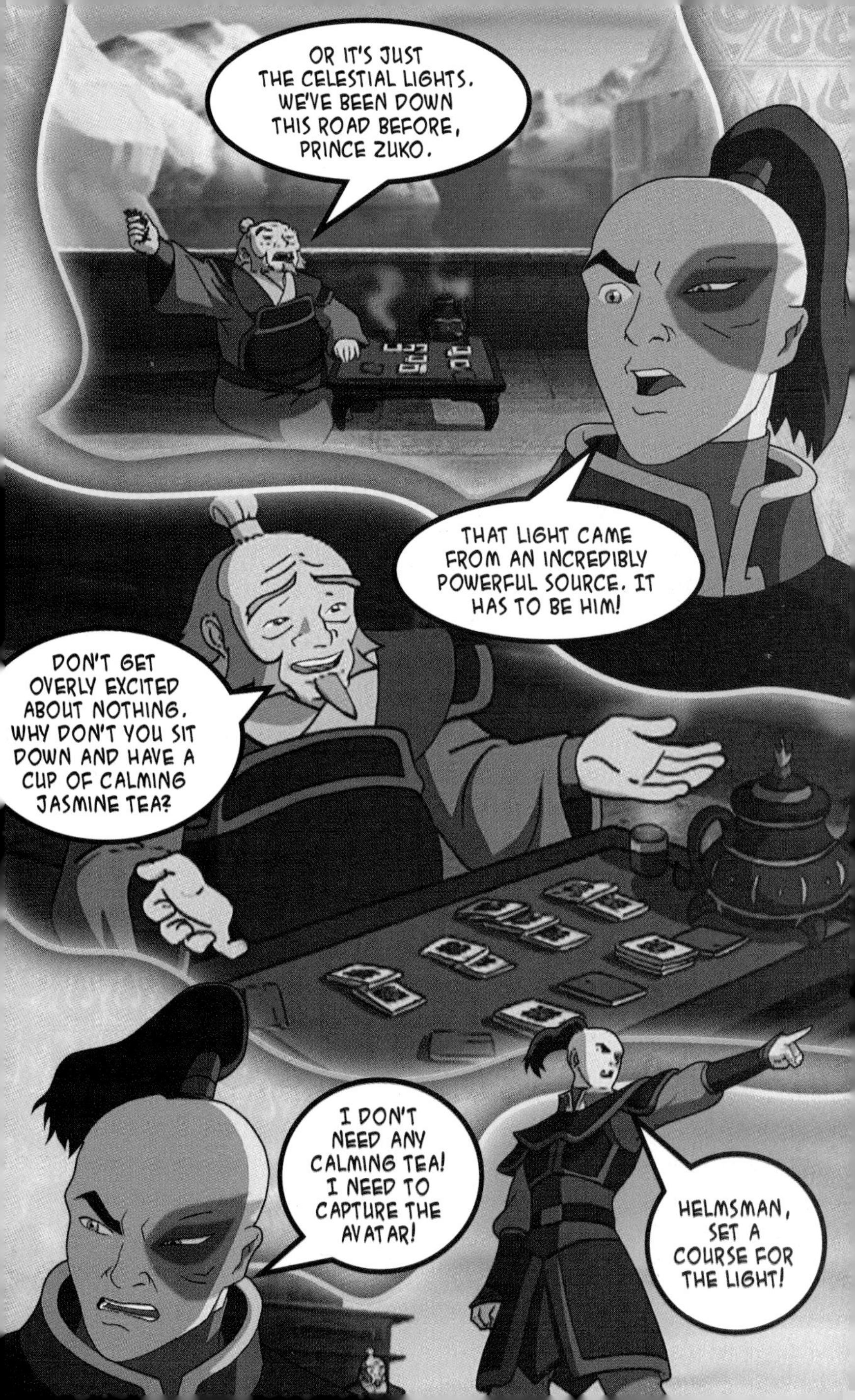
OR IT'S JUST THE CELESTIAL LIGHTS. WE'VE BEEN DOWN THIS ROAD BEFORE, PRINCE ZUKO.
THAT LIGHT CAME FROM AN INCREDIBLY POWERFUL SOURCE. IT HAS TO BE HIM!
DON'T GET OVERLY EXCITED ABOUT NOTHING. WHY DON'T YOU SIT DOWN AND HAVE A CUP OF CALMING JASMINE TEA?
I DON'T NEED ANY CALMING TEA! I NEED TO CAPTURE THE AVATAR!
HELMSMAN, SET A COURSE FOR THE LIGHT!

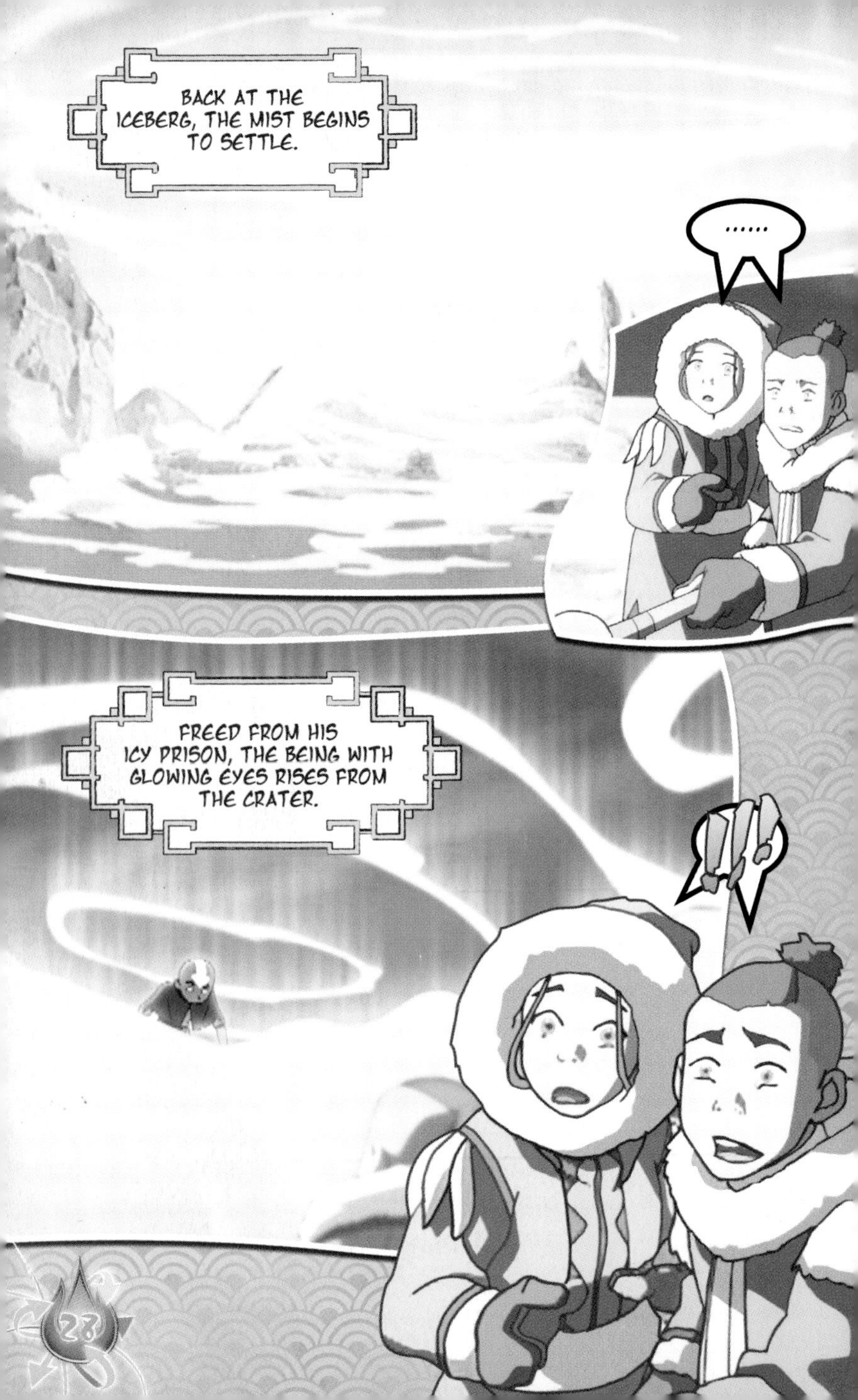

BACK AT THE ICEBERG, THE MIST BEGINS TO SETTLE.
......
FREED FROM HIS ICY PRISON, THE BEING WITH GLOWING EYES RISES FROM THE CRATER.
!!

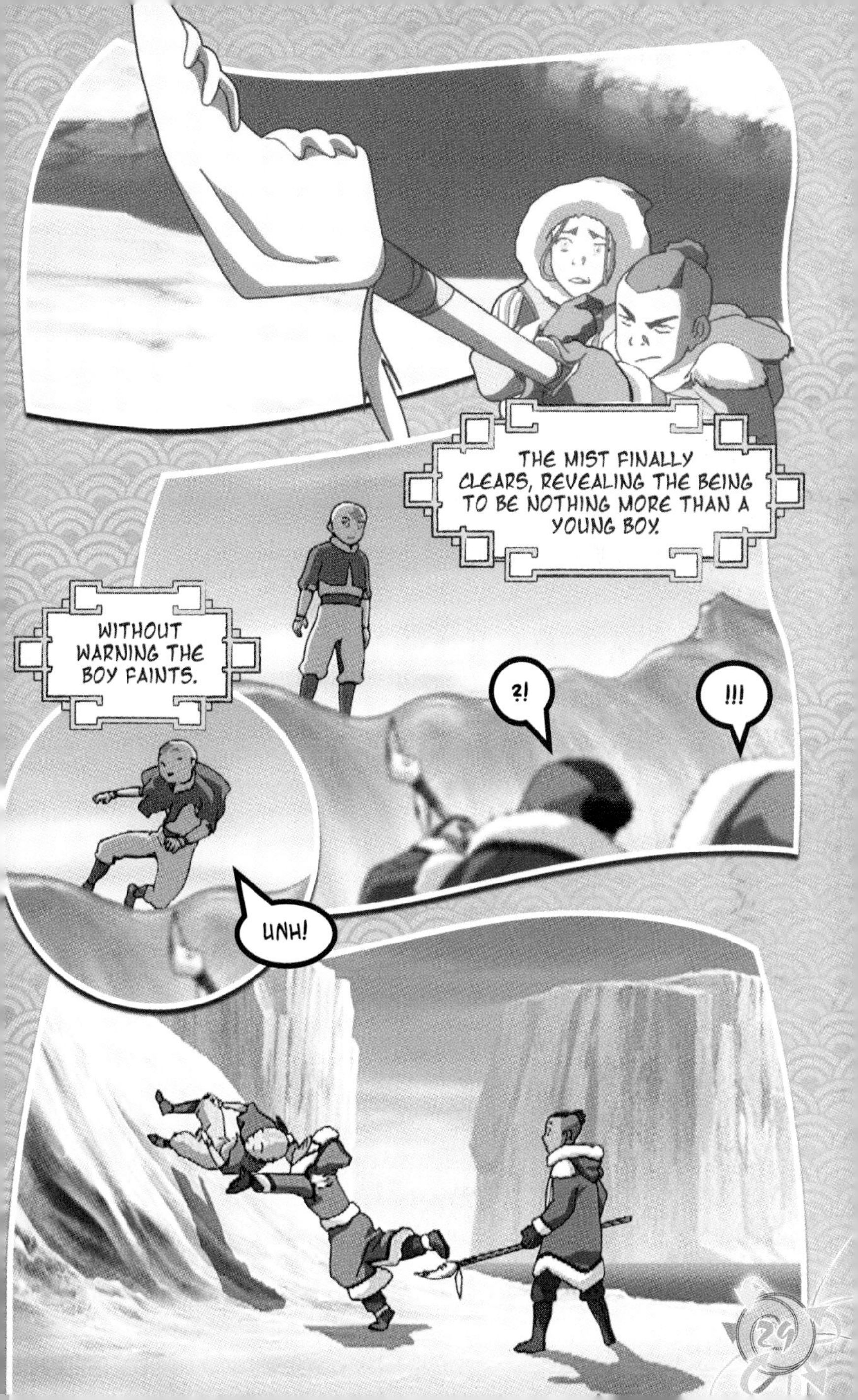
THE MIST FINALLY CLEARS, REVEALING THE BEING TO BE NOTHING MORE THAN A YOUNG BOY.
WITHOUT WARNING THE BOY FAINTS.
UNH!
?!
!!!

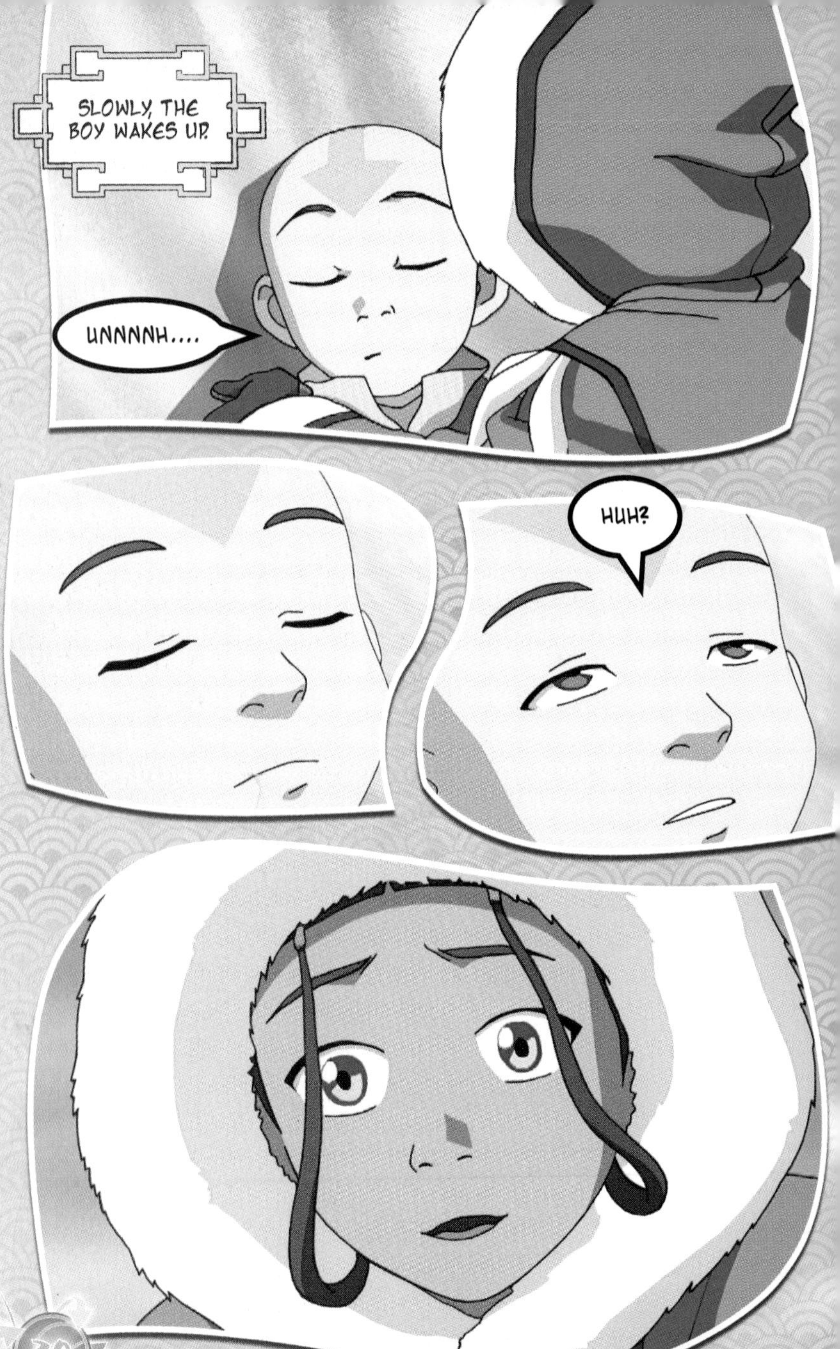
SLOWLY, THE BOY WAKES UP.
UNNNNH....
HUH?

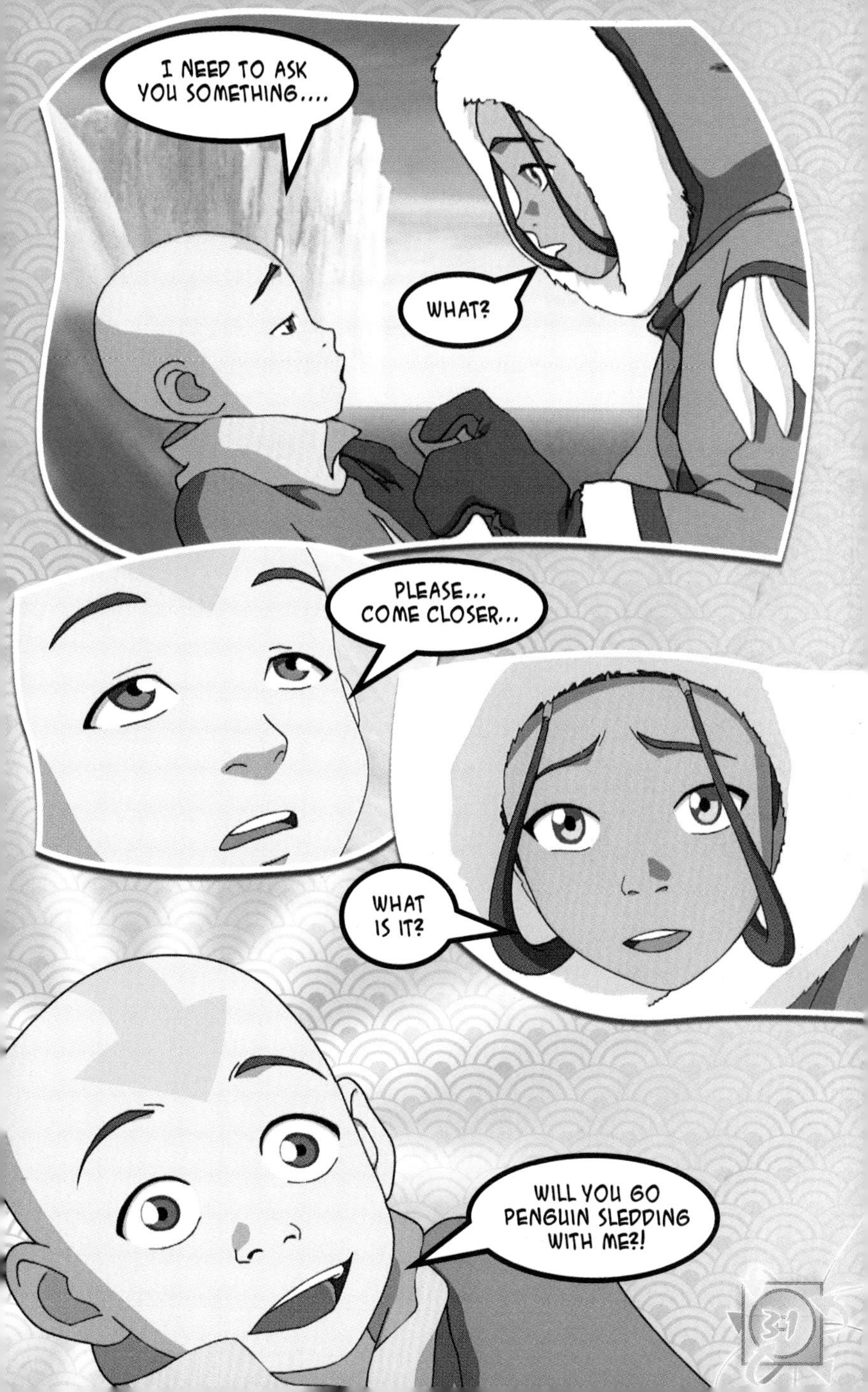
I NEED TO ASK YOU SOMETHING....
WHAT?
PLEASE... COME CLOSER...
WHAT IS IT?
WILL YOU GO PENGUIN SLEDDING WITH ME?!

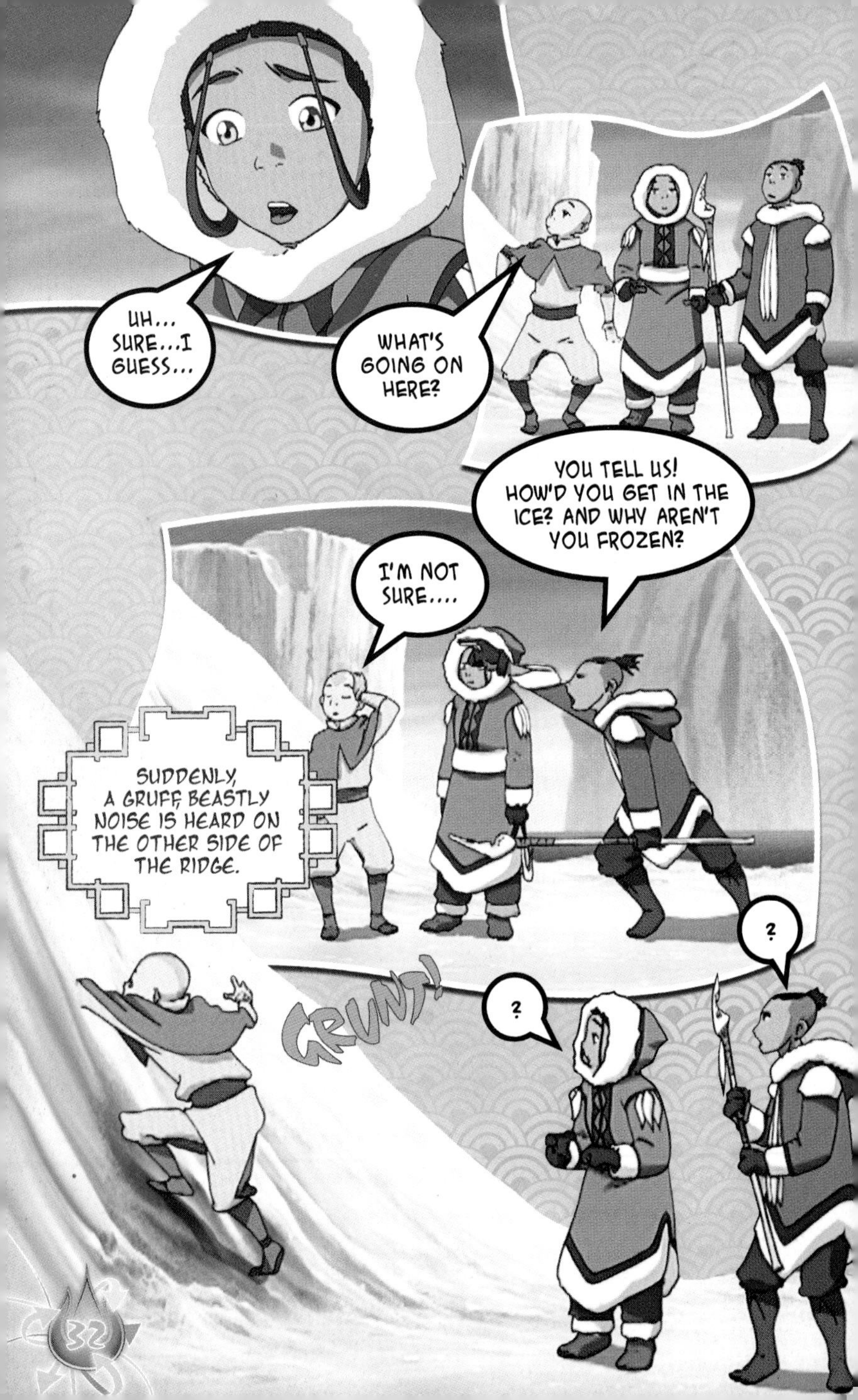
UH... SURE...I GUESS...
WHAT'S GOING ON HERE?
YOU TELL US! HOW'D YOU GET IN THE ICE? AND WHY AREN'T YOU FROZEN?
I'M NOT SURE....
SUDDENLY, A GRUFF, BEASTLY NOISE IS HEARD ON THE OTHER SIDE OF THE RIDGE.
GRUNT!
?
?

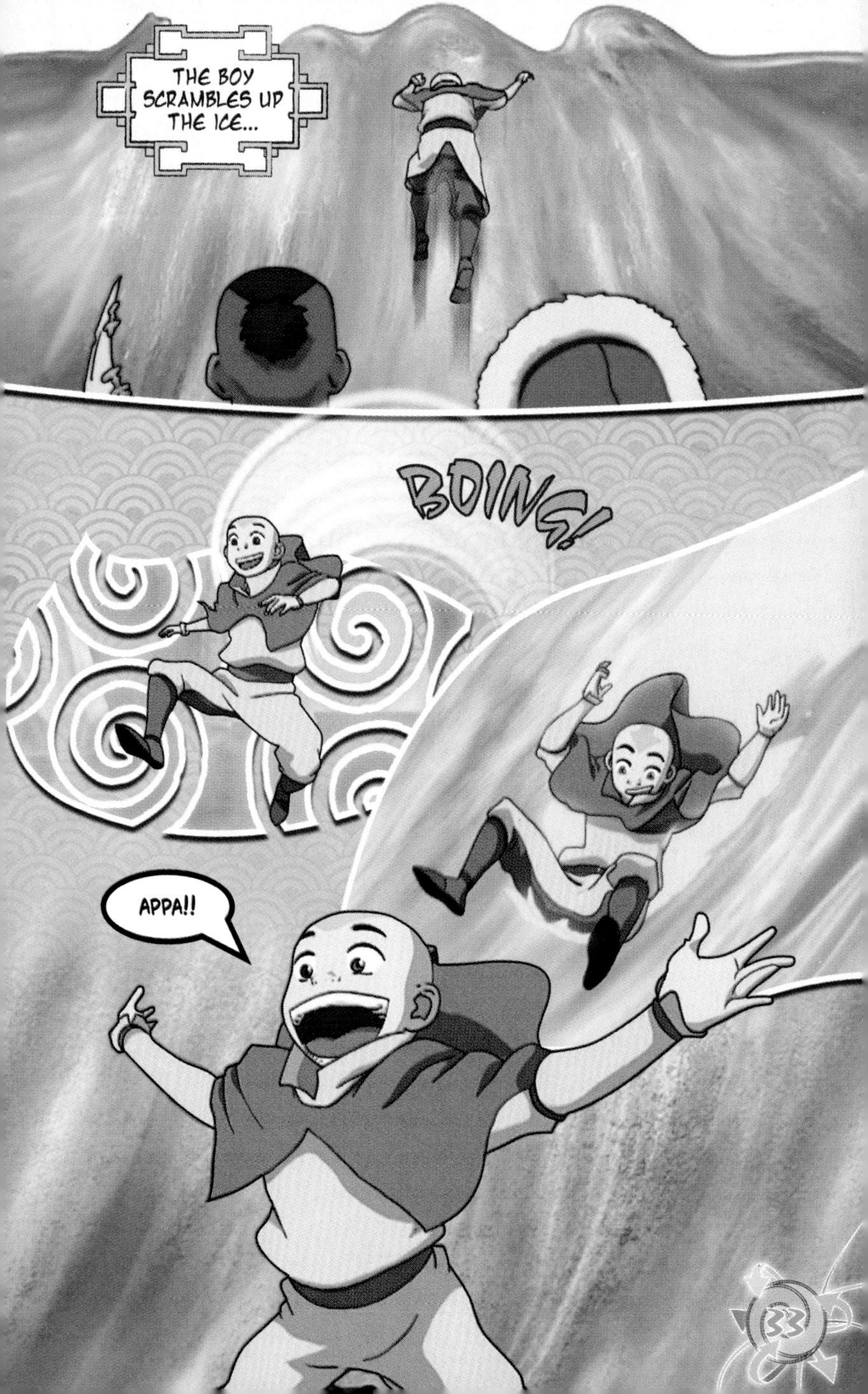
THE BOY SCRAMBLES UP THE ICE...
BOING!
APPA!!

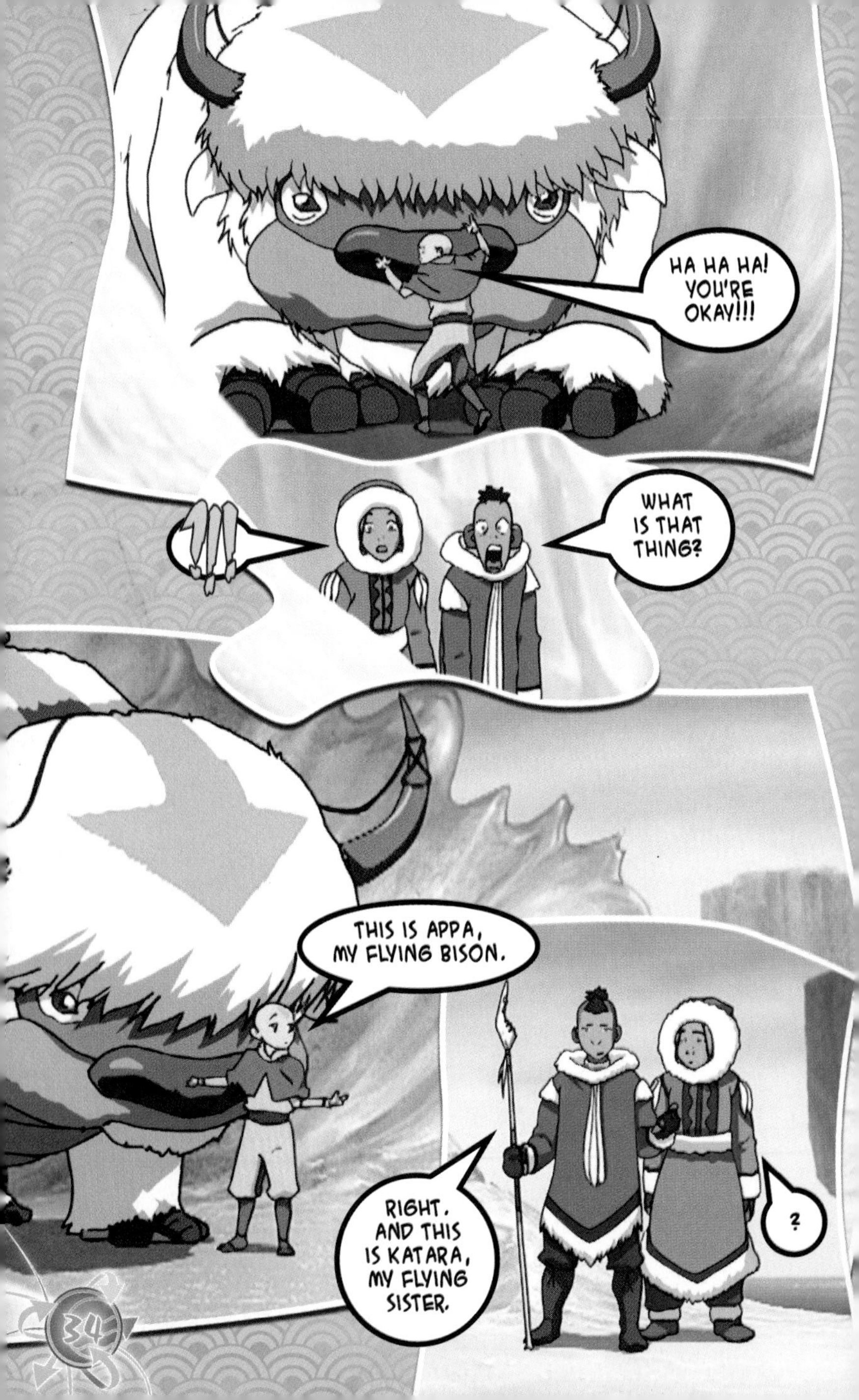
HA HA HA! YOU'RE OKAY!!!
WHAT IS THAT THING?
THIS IS APPA, MY FLYING BISON.
RIGHT. AND THIS IS KATARA, MY FLYING SISTER.
?
34

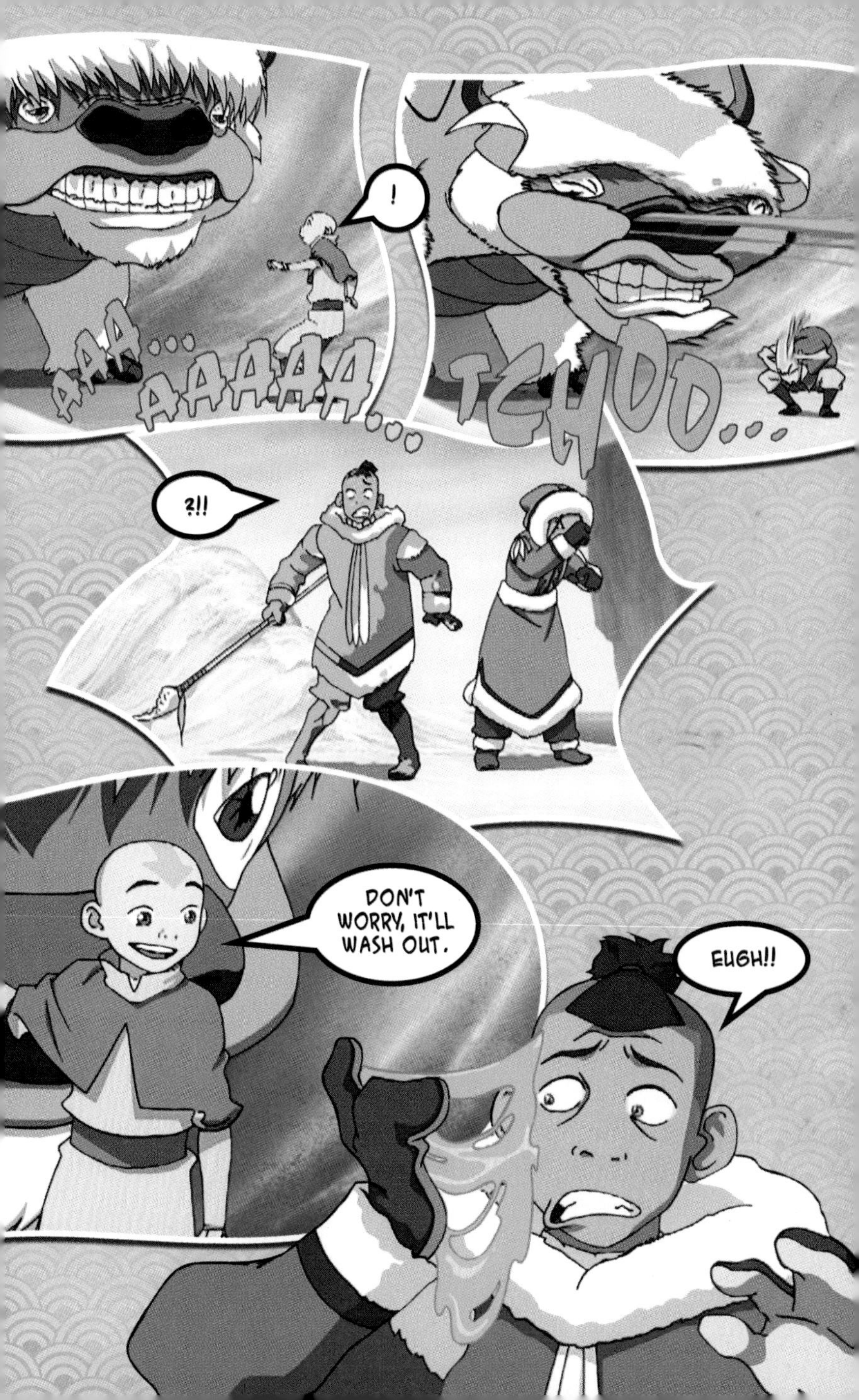
AAA...
AAAAA...
!
TCHOO...
?!!
DON'T WORRY, IT'LL WASH OUT.
EUGH!!

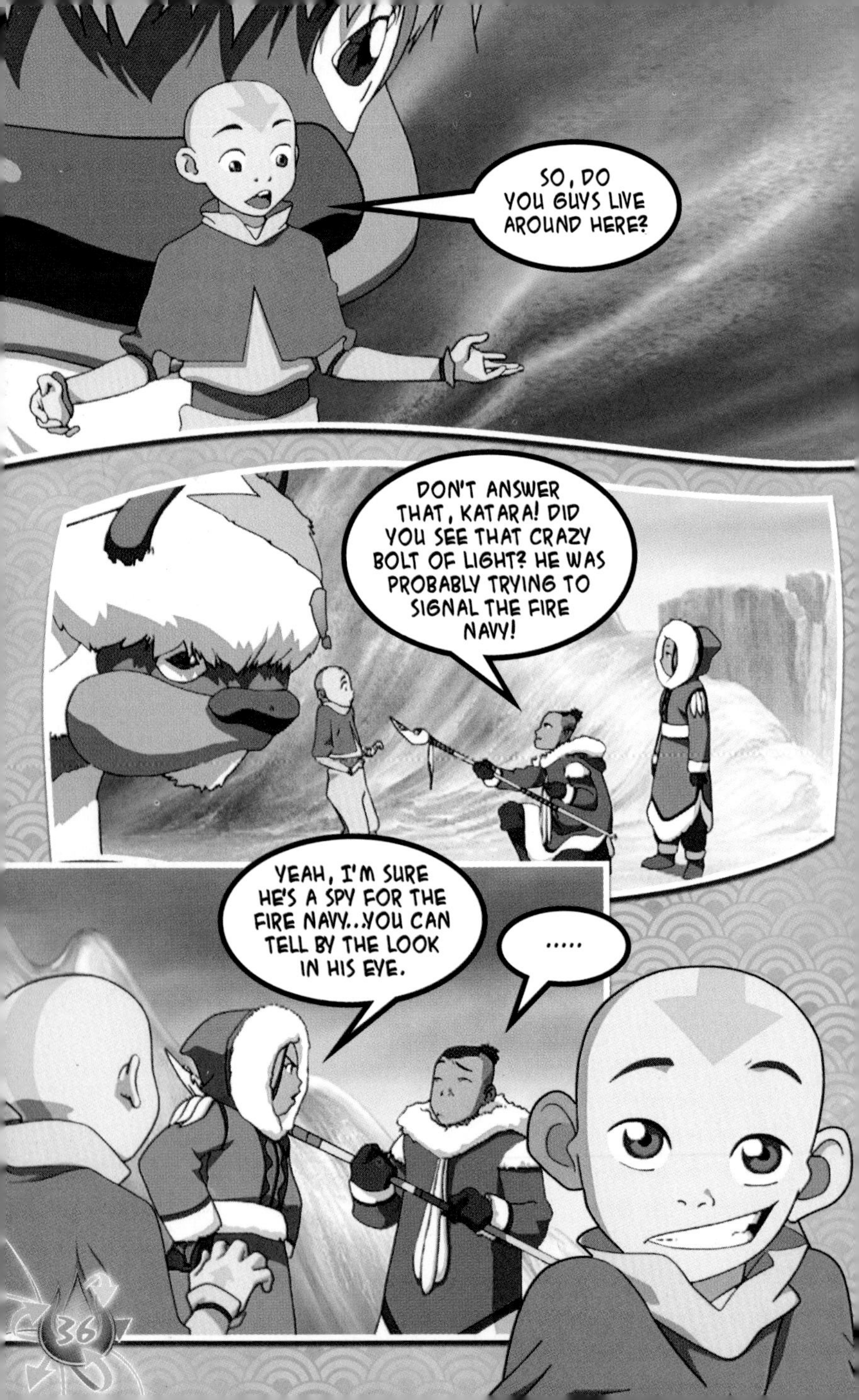
SO, DO YOU GUYS LIVE AROUND HERE?
DON'T ANSWER THAT, KATARA! DID YOU SEE THAT CRAZY BOLT OF LIGHT? HE WAS PROBABLY TRYING TO SIGNAL THE FIRE NAVY!
YEAH, I'M SURE HE'S A SPY FOR THE FIRE NAVY...YOU CAN TELL BY THE LOOK IN HIS EYE.
.....

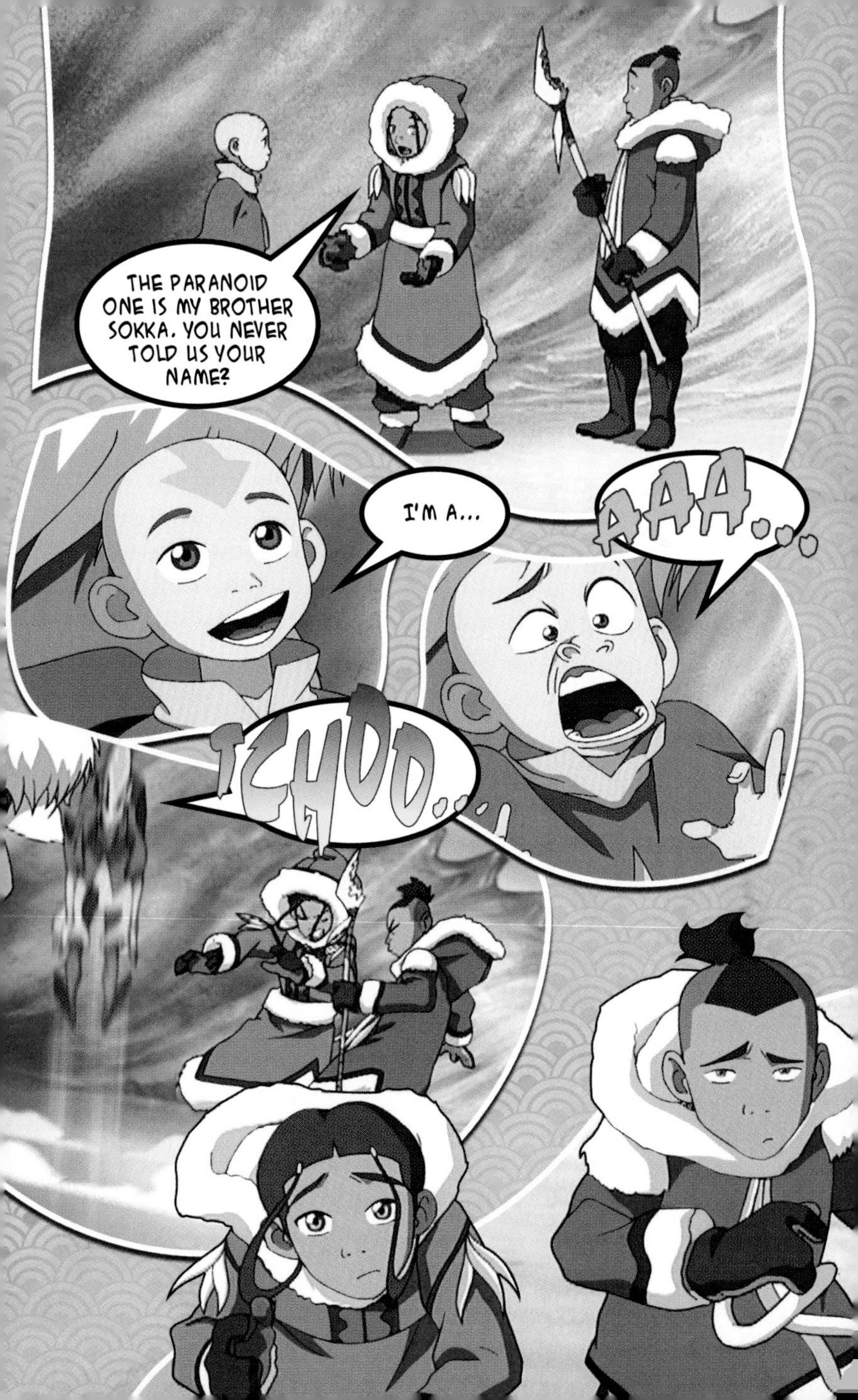
THE PARANOID ONE IS MY BROTHER SOKKA. YOU NEVER TOLD US YOUR NAME?
I'M A...
AAA...
TCHOO...

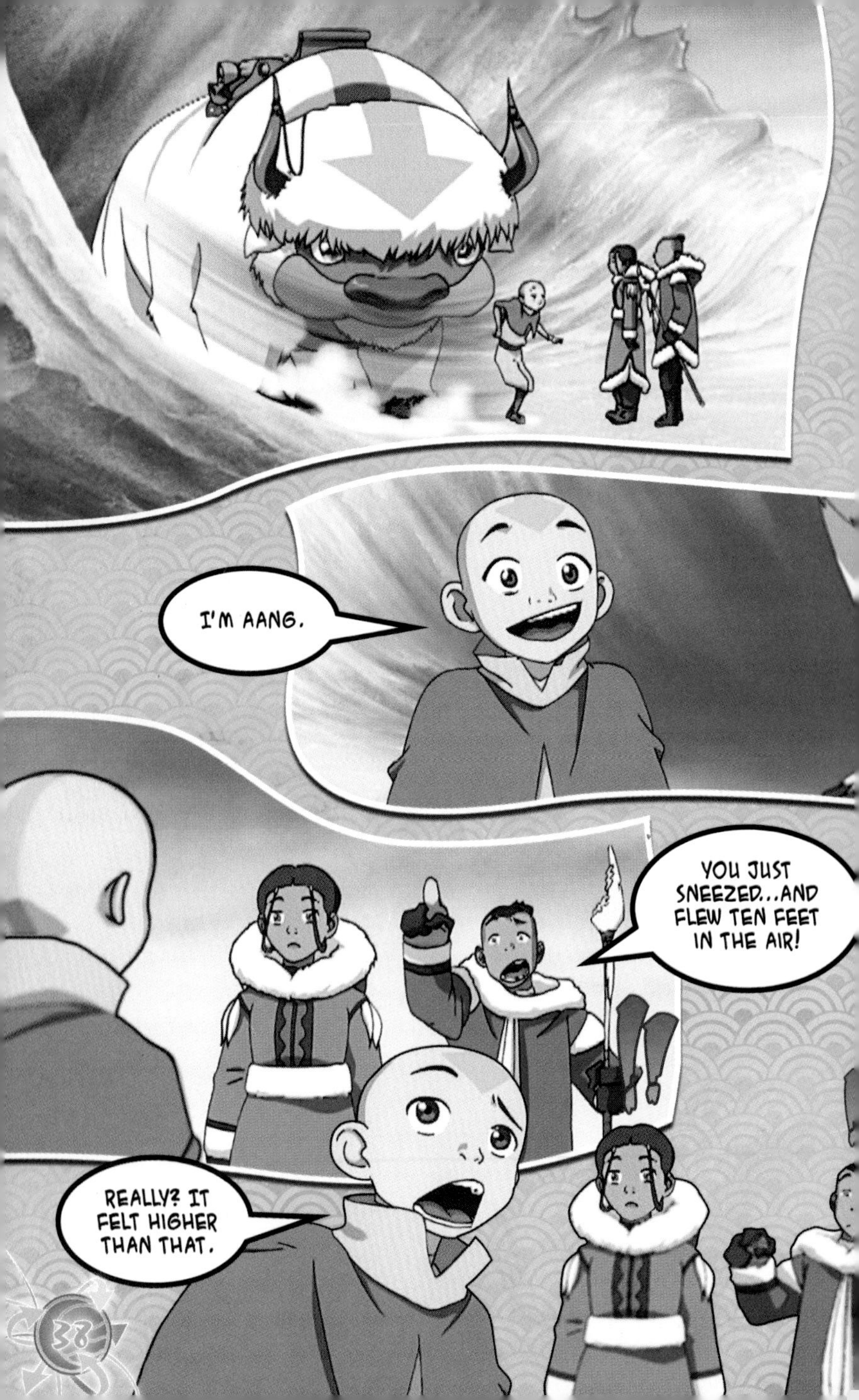
I'M AANG.
YOU JUST SNEEZED...AND FLEW TEN FEET IN THE AIR!
REALLY? IT FELT HIGHER THAN THAT.

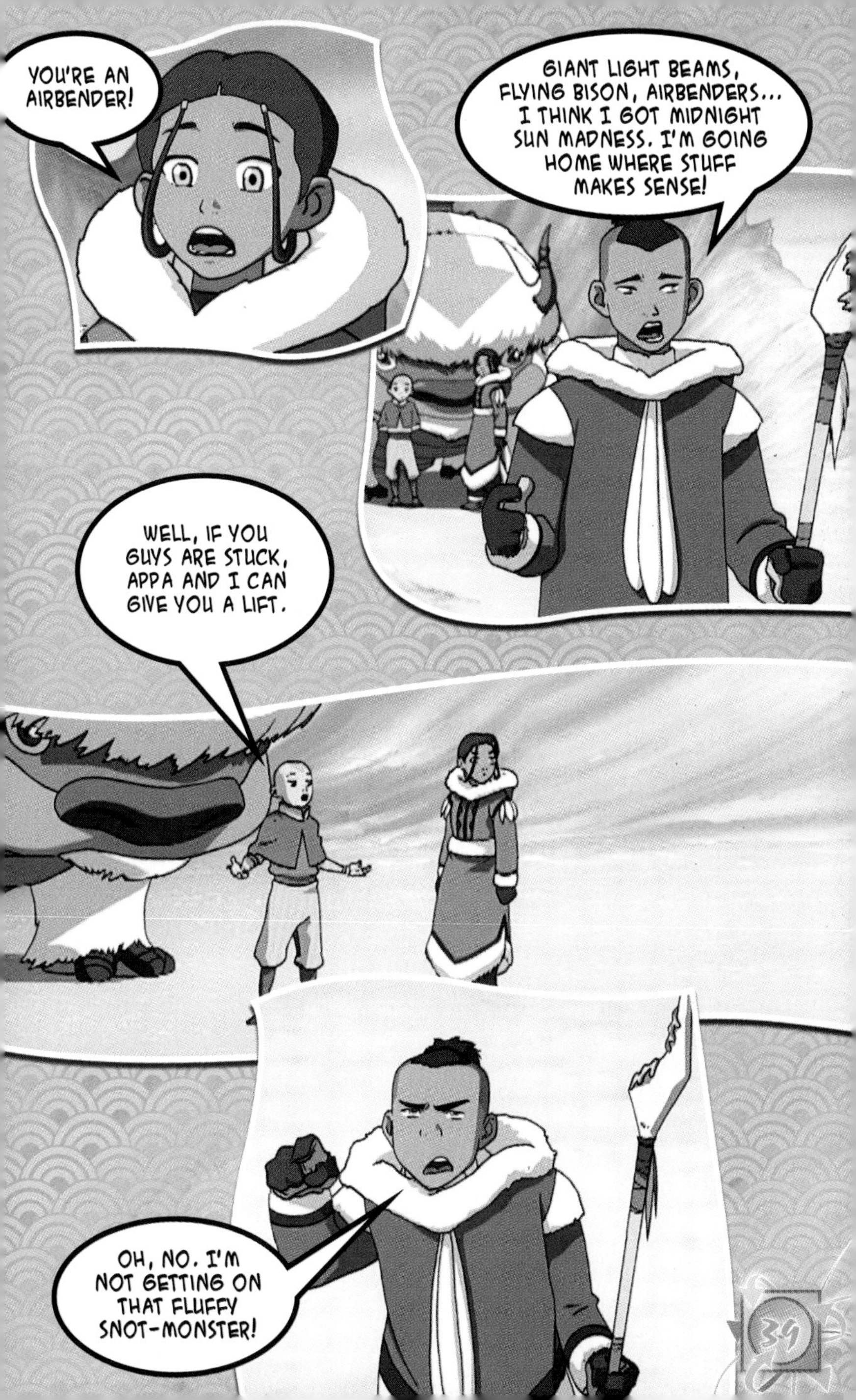
YOU'RE AN AIRBENDER!
GIANT LIGHT BEAMS, FLYING BISON, AIRBENDERS... I THINK I GOT MIDNIGHT SUN MADNESS. I'M GOING HOME WHERE STUFF MAKES SENSE!
WELL, IF YOU GUYS ARE STUCK, APPA AND I CAN GIVE YOU A LIFT.
OH, NO. I'M NOT GETTING ON THAT FLUFFY SNOT-MONSTER!

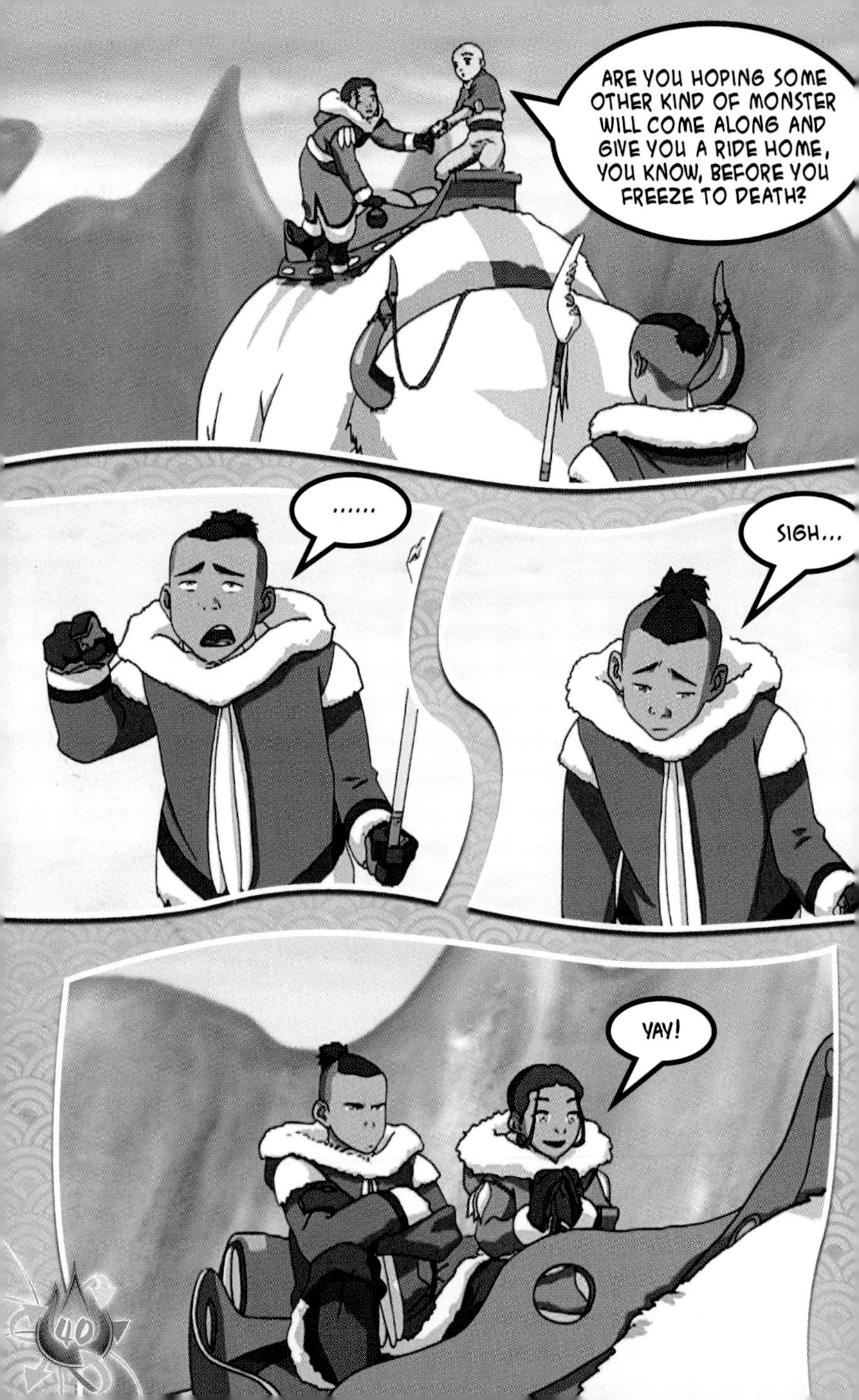
ARE YOU HOPING SOME OTHER KIND OF MONSTER WILL COME ALONG AND GIVE YOU A RIDE HOME, YOU KNOW, BEFORE YOU FREEZE TO DEATH?
......
SIGH...
YAY!

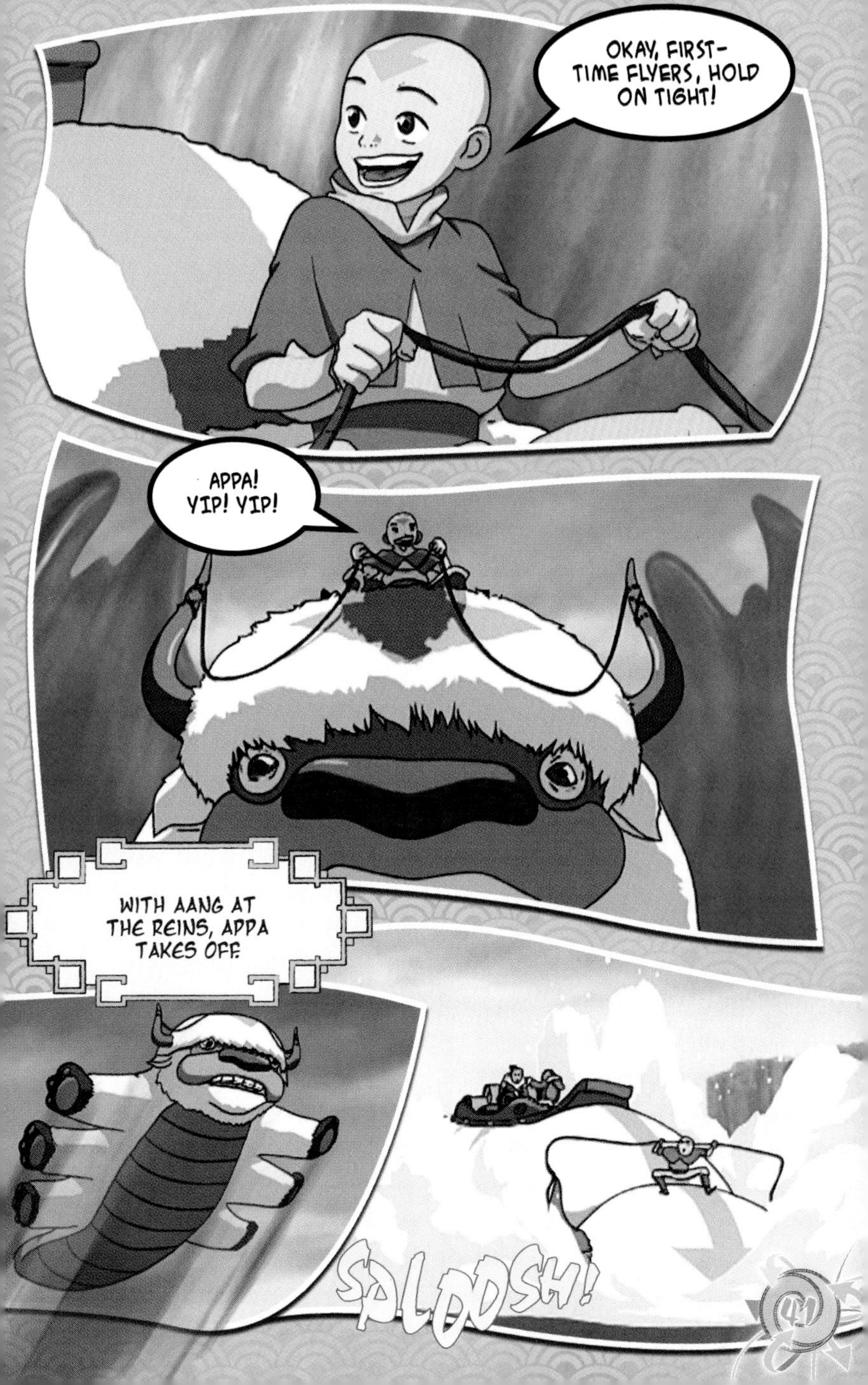
OKAY, FIRST-TIME FLYERS, HOLD ON TIGHT!
APPA! YIP! YIP!
WITH AANG AT THE REINS, APPA TAKES OFF.
SPLOOSH!

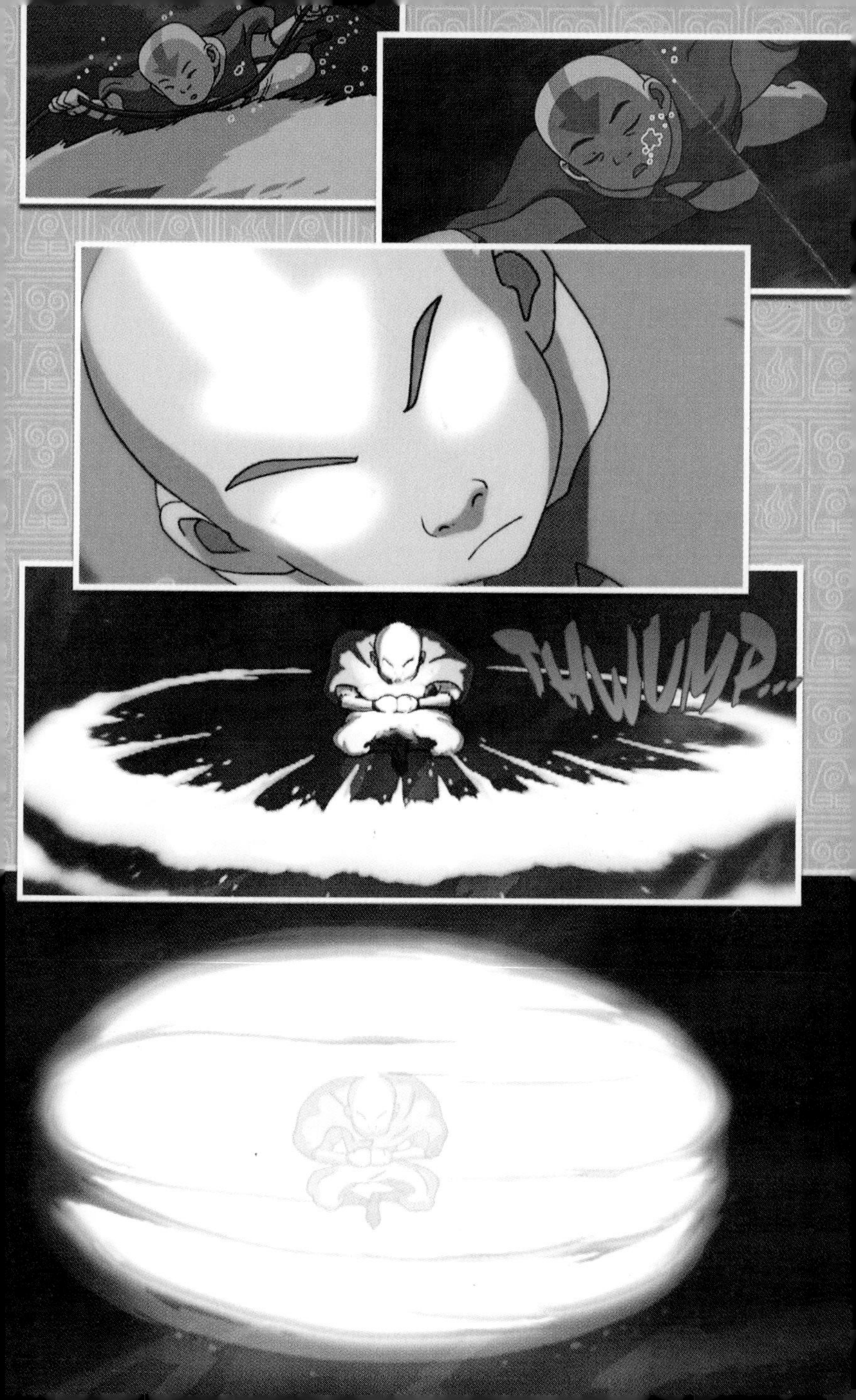
THWUMP...

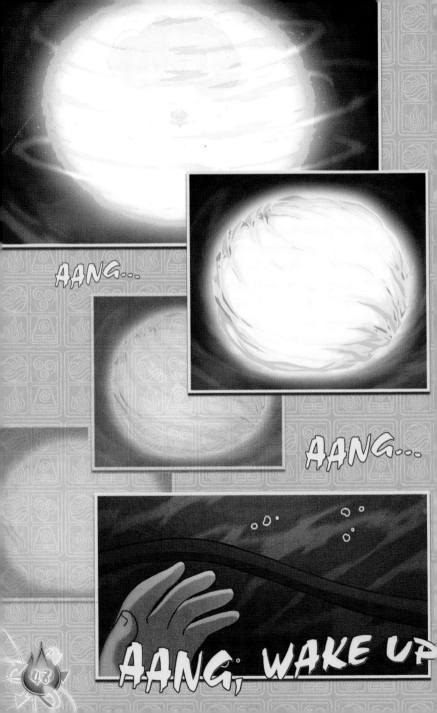

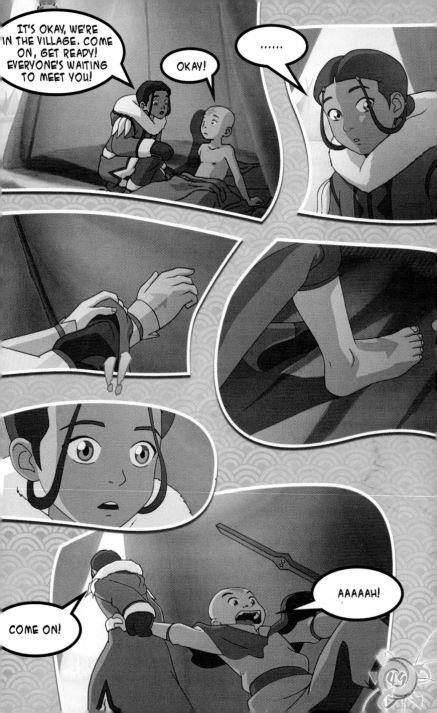

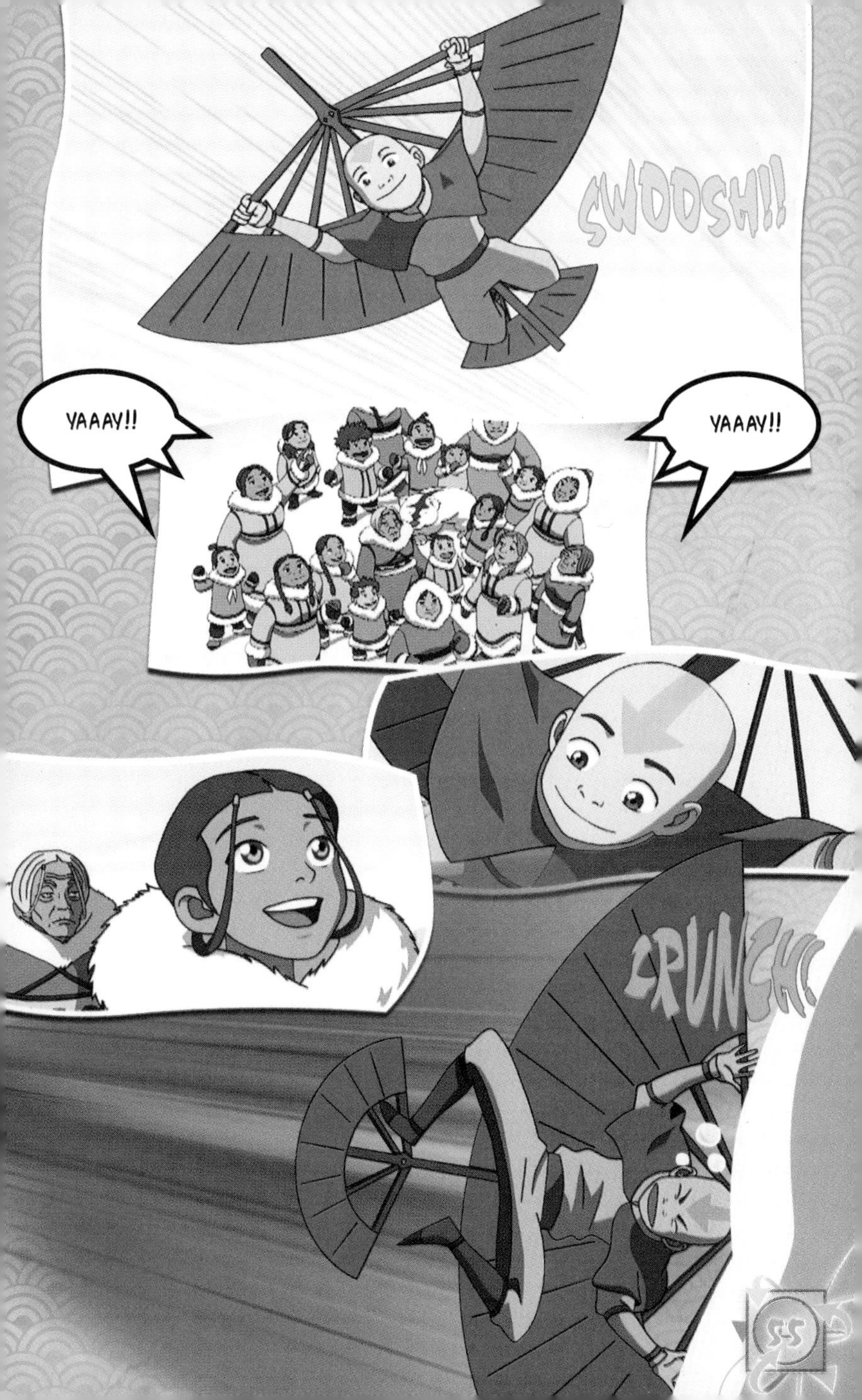
SWOOSH!!
YAAAY!!
YAAAY!!
CRUNCH!

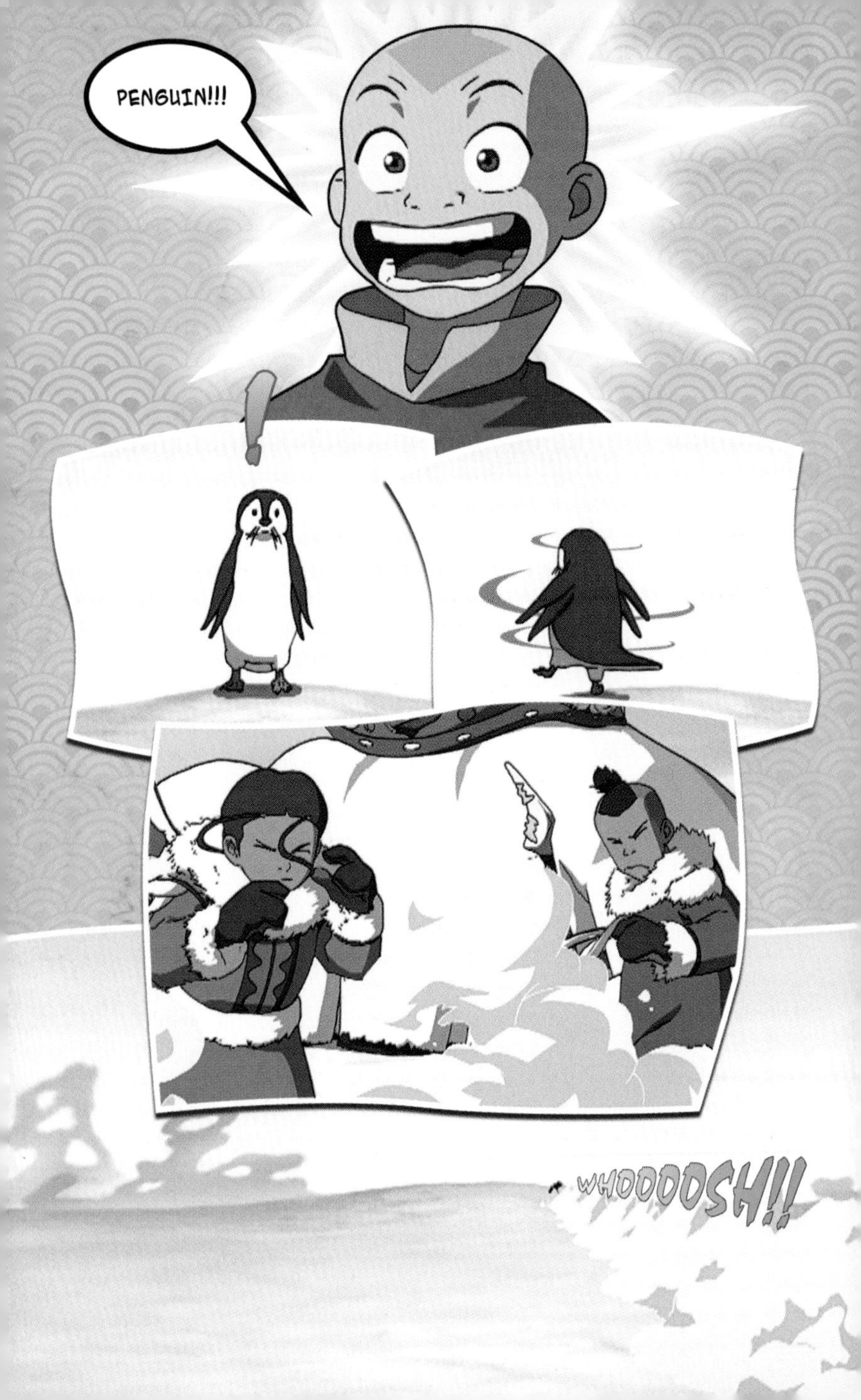
PENGUIN!!!
WHOOOOSH!!

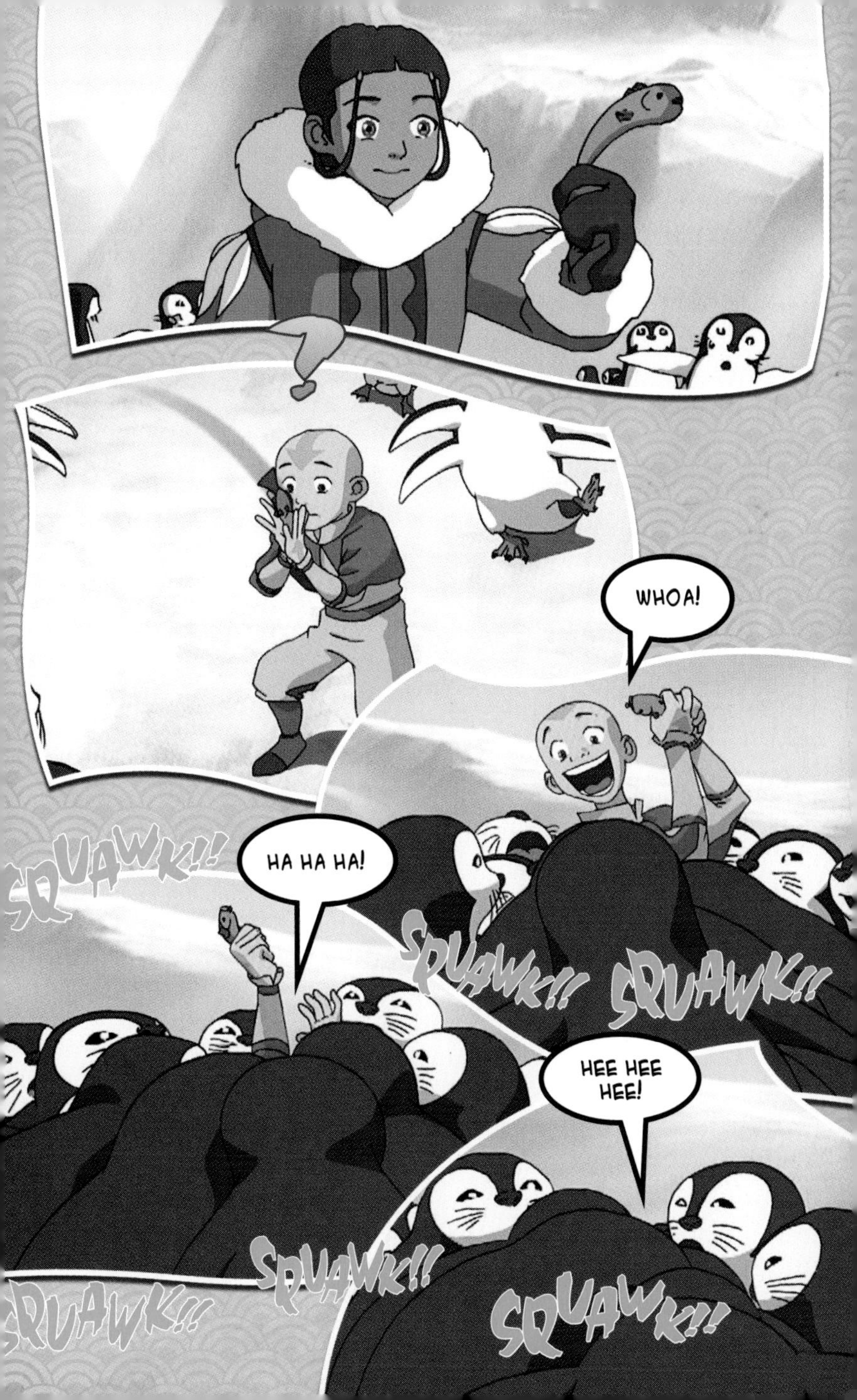
WHOA!
SQUAWK!!
HA HA HA!
SQUAWK!!
SQUAWK!!
HEE HEE HEE!
SQUAWK!!
SQUAWK!!
SQUAWK!!

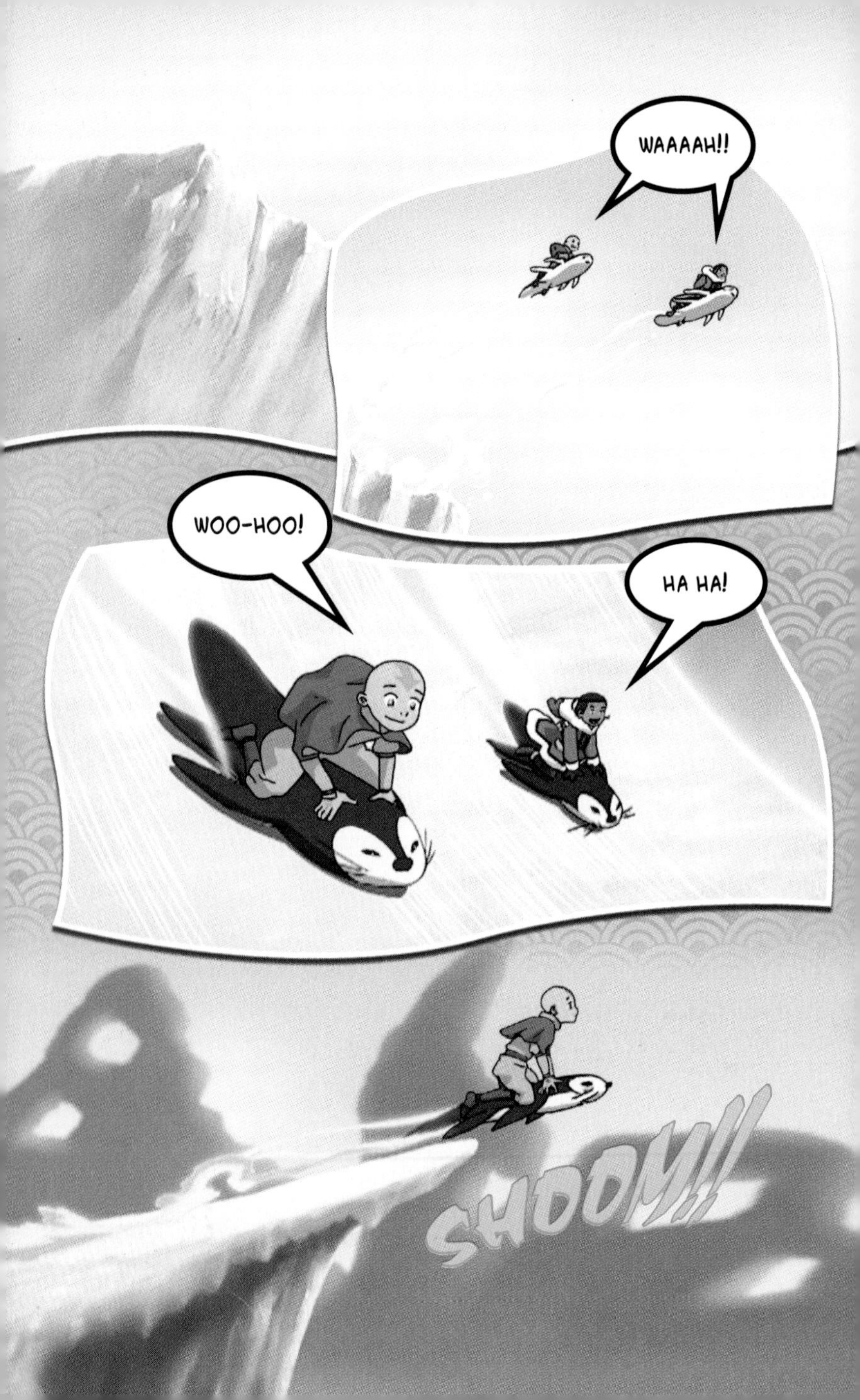
WAAAAH!!
WOO-HOO!
HA HA!
SHOOM!!

YEEAAAAAH!!
I HAVEN'T DONE THIS SINCE I WAS A KID!
YOU STILL **ARE** A KID!
WHOOOOSH!!

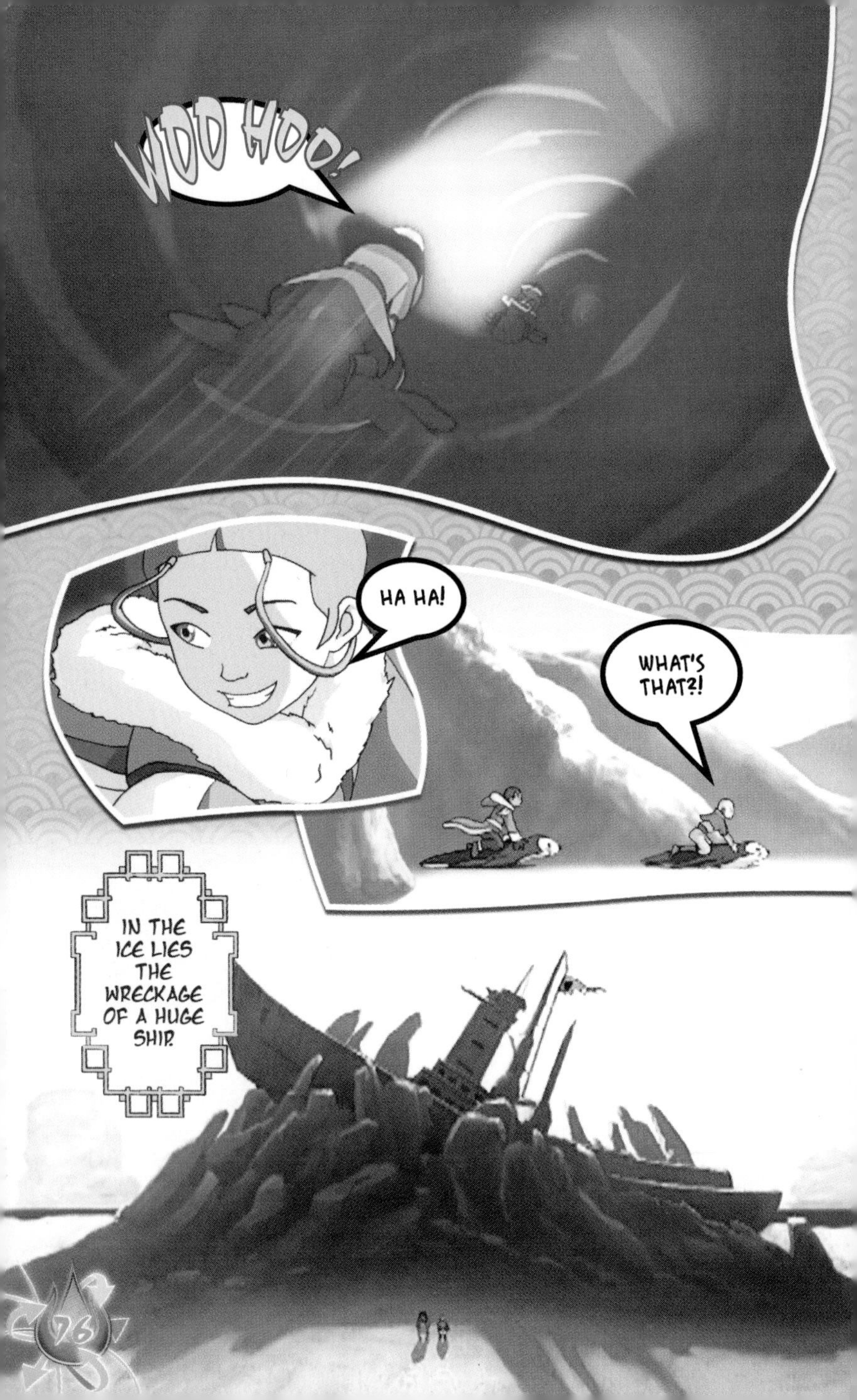
WOO HOO!
HA HA!
WHAT'S THAT?!
IN THE ICE LIES THE WRECKAGE OF A HUGE SHIP.

...THEIR FEET ON THE COLD METAL FLOORS...
CLANK!
CLANK!
CLANK!
...AND THE RATS.
SQUEAK!
SQUEAK!
EVENTUALLY, THE TWO ARRIVE IN THE ARMORY ROOM, FILLED WITH VICIOUS-LOOKING WEAPONS.
THIS SHIP HAS HAUNTED MY TRIBE SINCE GRAN-GRAN WAS A LITTLE GIRL. IT WAS PART OF THE FIRE NATION'S FIRST ATTACKS.

WATER TRIBES

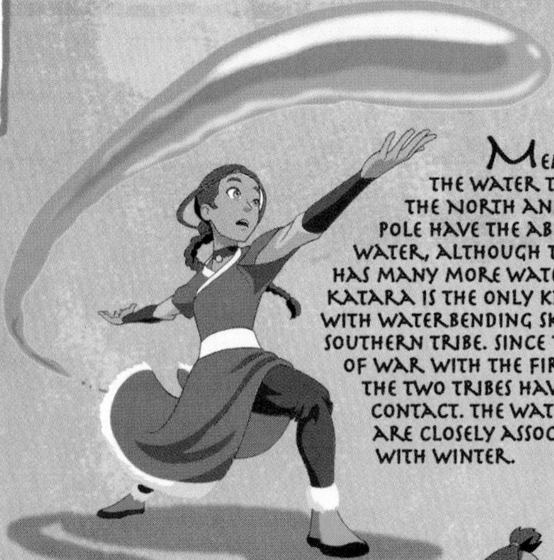

MEMBERS OF THE WATER TRIBES OF THE NORTH AND SOUTH POLE HAVE THE ABILITY TO BEND WATER, ALTHOUGH THE NORTH POL HAS MANY MORE WATERBENDERS. KATARA IS THE ONLY KNOWN PERSON WITH WATERBENDING SKILL IN THE SOUTHERN TRIBE. SINCE THE OUTBREAK OF WAR WITH THE FIRE NATION, THE TWO TRIBES HAVE NOT HAD CONTACT. THE WATER TRIBES ARE CLOSELY ASSOCIATED WITH WINTER.

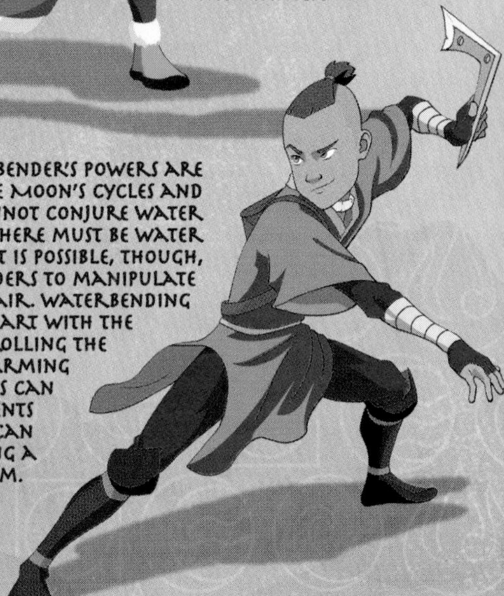

A WATERBENDER'S POWERS ARE STRENGTHENED BY THE MOON'S CYCLES AND THE RAIN. THEY CANNOT CONJURE WATER OUT OF THIN AIR, THERE MUST BE WATER AROUND THEM. IT IS POSSIBLE, THOUGH, FOR WATERBENDERS TO MANIPULATE MOISTURE IN THE AIR. WATERBENDING IS A DEFENSIVE ART WITH THE INTENTION OF CONTROLLING THE OPPONENT, NOT HARMING HIM. WATERBENDERS CAN ENCASE THEIR OPPONENTS IN BLOCKS OR THEY CAN ESCAPE BY CREATING A SHEET OF STEAM.

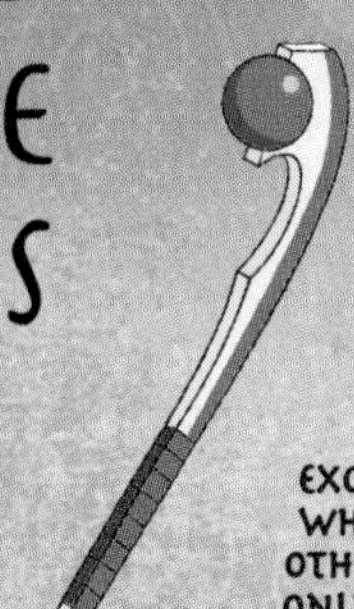

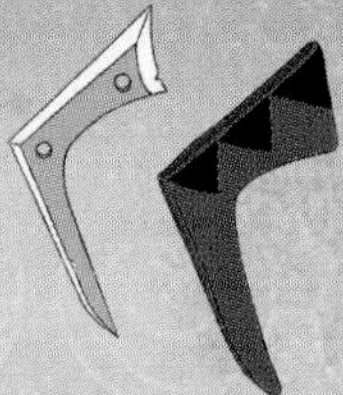

NOT EVERYBODY HAS THE ABILITY TO BEND. THIS IS TRUE OF ALL THE NATIONS WITH THE ONE EXCEPTION BEING THE AIR NOMADS, WHO ARE ALL AIRBENDERS. IN THE OTHER NATIONS, BENDERS MAKE UP ONLY A SMALL PERCENTAGE OF THE PEOPLE. MEMBERS OF THE WATER TRIBE WHO DO NOT POSSESS BENDING SKILLS USE BOOMERANGS AND STAFFS AS WEAPONS.

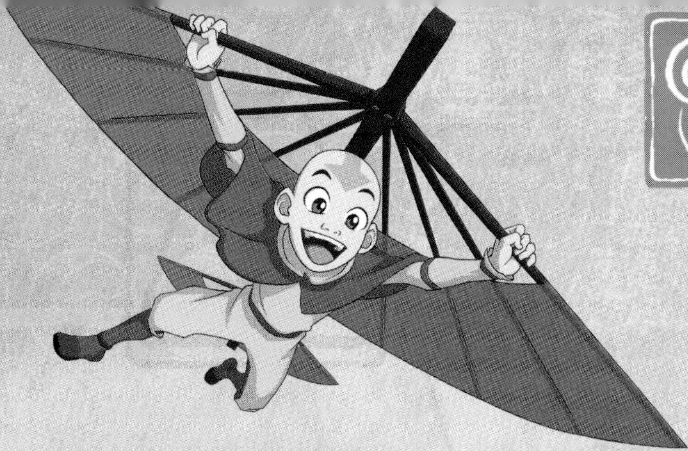

AIR NOMADS

The air nomads travel the world on flying bison, like Appa, but are based at one of four main air temples: North, South, East or West. Some air nomads live in the temples. The air nomads are a peaceful people and are the most spiritually enlightened of all the nations. They were also the first people to be attacked by the Fire Nation at the beginning of the war. They have not been seen for hundreds of years and are believed to be extinct. The air nomads are closely associated with autumn.

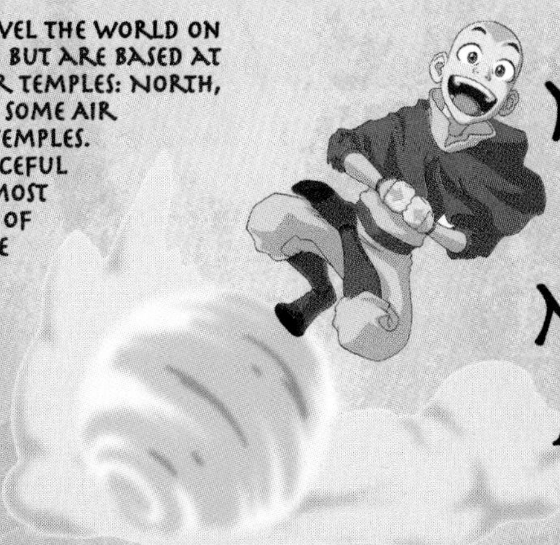

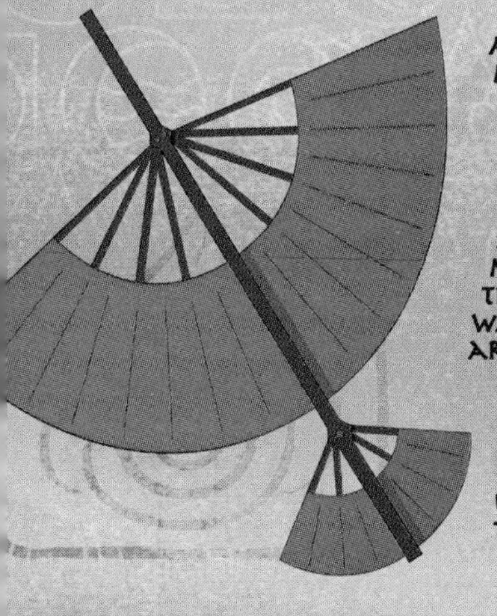

Airbenders cannot fly. They manipulate air currents to enhance their normal movements. As a result, airbenders can jump higher, run faster and move quicker than other benders. Aang is an extremely skilled airbender. Being the Avatar means that he is the only person in the world who can also bend fire, water and earth, although his skills are not developed in these areas.

Although airbenders cannot fly, they can ride on air currents using their staffs, which transform into gliders.

FIRE NATION

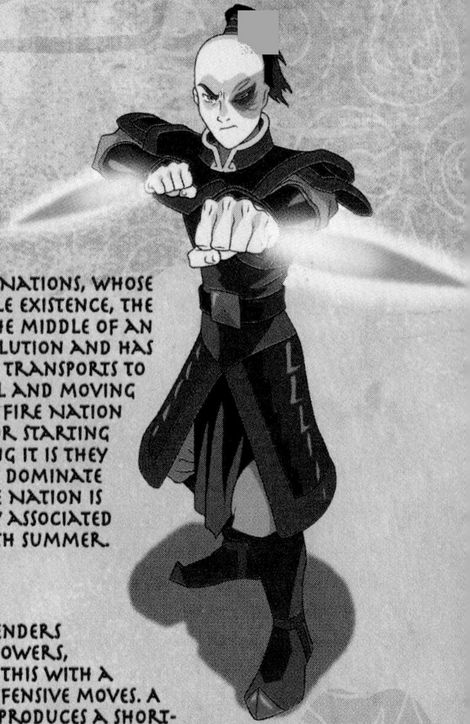

Unlike the air, earth and water nations, whose people lead a simple existence, the Fire Nation is in the middle of an industrial revolution and has steam-powered transports to help with travel and moving supplies. It is the Fire Nation who is responsible for starting the war, believing it is they who should rightly dominate the world. The Fire Nation is closely associated with summer.

Although firebenders lack defensive powers, they make up for this with a wide variety of offensive moves. A quick jab or kick produces a short-range burst of flame. Whirlwind and spinning kicks produce blazing arcs and rings of fire that explode in all directions with punches creating fireballs. If a number of firebenders combine their power, they can create missiles of flame that can fly over long distances with devastating effects. Although they possess terrifying powers, firebenders have their weaknesses. Their power is influenced by the sun.

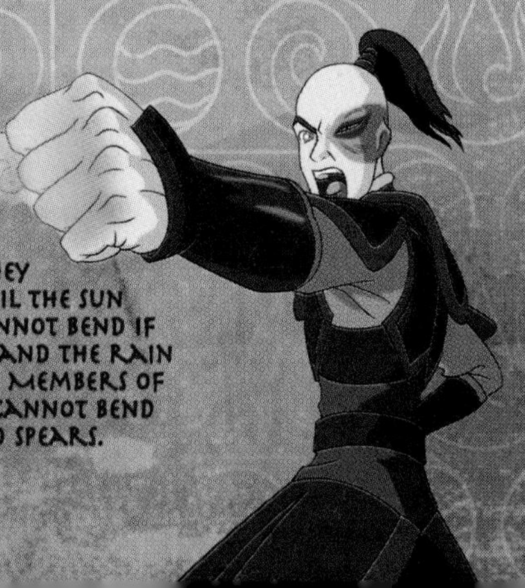

If there is an eclipse, they lose their powers until the sun returns. They also cannot bend if they are underwater, and the rain weakens their powers. Members of the Fire Nation who cannot bend carry swords and spears.

EARTH KINGDOM

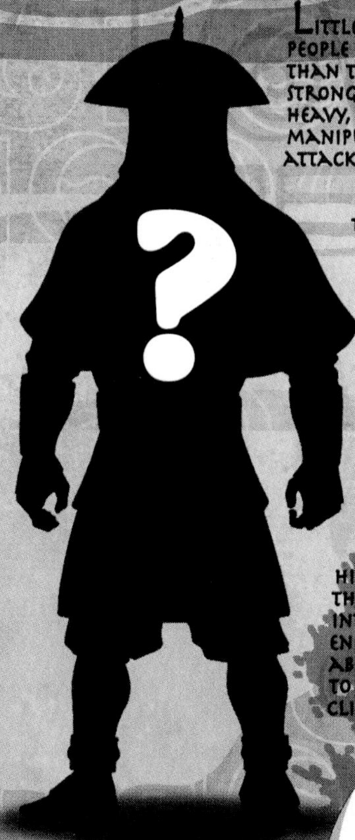

Little is known about the people of this nation other than they are a proud and strong people. Using their heavy, muscular bodies, they manipulate the ground for attack and defense.

They can knock an enemy off his feet by pounding the ground, creating a small earthquake. They can also use the earth to catapult them into the air to avoid attacks and create fissures in the ground to swallow enemies. Other moves include raising stone slabs from the ground for offense and defense, as well as levitating and throwing rocks.

High-level earthbenders have the power to turn the ground into quicksand to trap their enemies. Earthbenders are also able to magnetize their limbs to stone, which allows them to climb walls and cliffs. The Earth Kingdom is closely associated with spring.

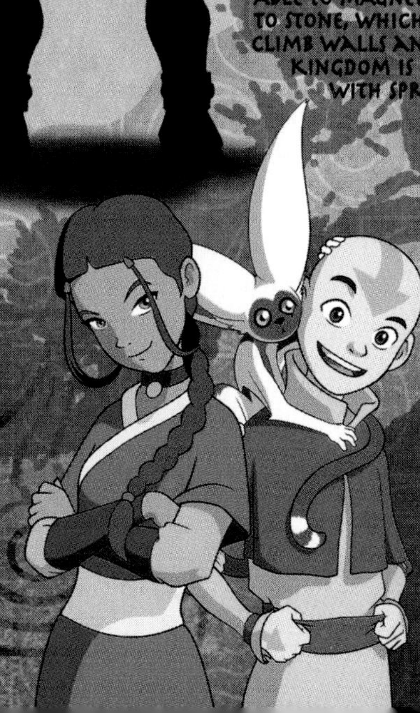

SEE YOU NEXT TIME!

BUSTiN' OUT FROM BiKiNi BOTTOM!

SPONGEBOB'S GOT HiS OWN CINE-MANGA™

AVAILABLE NOW AT YOUR FAVORITE BOOKSTORE

™ 2003 VIACOM INTERNATIONAL INC. ALL RIGHTS RESERVED. NICKELODEON, SPONGEBOB SQUAREPANTS
AND ALL RELATED TITLES, LOGOS AND CHARACTERS ARE TRADEMARKS OF VIACOM INTERNATIONAL INC.
TOKYOPOP IS A REGISTERED TRADEMARK OF MIXX ENTERTAINMENT, INC.

www.TOKYOPOP.com